# GROWING CHURCHES SINGAPORE STYLE

## Ministry in an Urban Context

### Keith W. Hinton

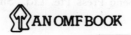
AN OMF BOOK

Overseas Missionary Fellowship
1058 Avenue Road
Toronto, Ontario M5N 2C6

Copyright © Overseas Missionary Fellowship
(formerly China Inland Mission)

First published ...... 1985

ISBN 9971-972-24-7

OMF BOOKS are distributed by OMF, 404 South Church
Street, Robesonia, Pa., 19551, USA; OMF, Belmont, The Vine,
Sevenoaks, Kent TN13 3TZ, UK; OMF, P.O. Box 177, Kew
East, Victoria 3102, Australia, and other OMF offices.

Published by **Overseas Missionary Fellowship (IHQ) Ltd.,**
2 Cluny Road, Singapore 1025, Republic of Singapore, and
printed by Hiap Seng Press Pte. Ltd., Singapore.

# Contents

# Preface

A vision without a task is a dream, a task without a vision is a
drudgery, but a vision and a task together radiate life and hope.
Many pastors, while serving faithfully in their parishes, are weary
with well-doing. Their tread is heavy and their ministry a burden
because they lack vision, direction and hope. It is my prayer
that this study will serve to inspire visions, to broaden the
horizons of possibility and to provide the practical materials
out of which a path may be cut directly to their realization.

This book then is offered to the church in Singapore with
the sincere desire that it will stimulate Christians of all denominations to more creative thinking and believing prayer as they
plan for the on-going development and growth of their congregations.

Because of the limitation of length, many aspects of growth
and culture are necessarily dealt with only briefly. I am well
aware that some of the areas touched upon require a good deal
more thought and discussion. It is my hope, therefore, that these
tentative ideas and suggestions will trigger the production of
further contributions by local writers for the benefit of the
church.

While this book is intended primarily for Singapore, the cultural
characteristics and principles outlined could well have a wider
application throughout Asia and, in particular, wherever there
are English-speaking Chinese churches growing in an urban
context.

I wish to acknowledge with gratitude the help received from
Dr. C. Peter Wagner, Dr. Bobby E. K. Sng, Rev. Howard Peskett
and Dr. Tay Eng Soon who read the completed manuscript and
offered many valuable criticisms and suggestions for its improvement. My special thanks go to my wife Linnet, my most faithful
critic, devoted editor and secretary. Without her help and constant encouragement, this book would never have seen the light
of day.

# Foreword

As the Church Growth Movement matures, the technology for researching and analyzing the growth of churches continues to improve. Keith Hinton's fascinating book on the dynamics of the growth of churches in Singapore is a state of the art document. It brings together in a concise and convincing way the major cluster of factors which influence the growth of churches both positively and negatively. When Hinton studied in the Fuller Seminary School of World Mission he became the recipient of the coveted Donald A. McGavran Church Growth Award, indication enough that he is eminently qualified to produce a book such as this.

As a first step, Keith Hinton describes the contextual factors which have influenced the churches in Singapore. This is significant because Singapore is only 25 years old as an independent nation. It is one of many newly created countries in today's world. And in many ways it is a model of sound government, a well functioning social order, and economic well being. How do these conditions affect the church? What about the sharp distinctions between large ethnic blocks? How does Christianity confront traditional religions? Can an understanding of urban anthropology aid the planning of strategy for the spread of the Gospel? These and many more questions are skilfully addressed in this book.

And then come the institutional factors. I am particularly impressed by Hinton's treatment of church leadership and how it relates to growth. He sees clearly that the pastor as equipper, rather than the outmoded model of pastor as enabler, is what is making a difference in the Singapore churches. He speaks of renewal, of church diseases which need special attention, and how parochial schools can influence growth. This is all tied up finally in a sound section on strategy planning.

I commend this book to all church leaders who are called by God to be a part of the spreading of the Gospel in Singapore, Southeast Asia and the surrounding regions. I also commend it to students of missiology and church growth from any continent. Our knowledge of how churches grow has been greatly advanced by this very significant work.

C. Peter Wagner
Fuller Seminary School of World Mission
Pasadena, California

# Chapter 1
# Introduction

## Singapore

An island with an energetic Chinese majority who refuse to
live according to the "rhythm of the tropics." There is a disturbing
sense of psychological incongruity which any visitor would notice,
between 85 degrees Fahrenheit – 85[%] humidity and 16 hours
hard work a day .... The whole island is covered with disciplined
"worker ants". It is a show case of nation building. It is an island
of efficiency in an ocean of South East Asian inefficiency. Singapore
(Lion City) is not a lion that eats and sleeps .... [with] a strong
teleologically, "eschatologically" minded political leadership. The
Kingdom of God, Singapore style, is just around the corner! ....
This is an amazing achievement! (Koyama 1974:4).

But life was not always so for this 19 year old, 618 square
kilometre island republic. On 9 August 1965, Singapore's two
year honeymoon as part of the Federation of Malaysia abruptly
ended: she was expelled, her Chinese majority recognized as a
threat to Malay supremacy. As a new, independent nation, her
life hung by a thread and the prophets foretold disaster.

The island was one of the most densely populated areas in
the world with most of her people living in a huge, squalid
slum. She had no natural hinterland, no natural resources, inadequate domestic markets to allow for the development of

industry, chronic unemployment and widespread corruption and vice.

Her existence was further jeopardized by the formidable pluralism of society that inhibited communication, fed misunderstanding and fomented suspicion. The ethnic cleavages correlated largely with socio-economic cleavages and frequently caused emotions to run high. The Chinese represented 77 per cent of the population. Many of these had grown rich through trading favours from the British. Malays and Indians, 15 and 7 per cent respectively, were mostly less privileged. These simple divisions obscure the complex heterogeneity of the population. For instance, the Chinese further divided into five major dialect groups — Hokkien, Teochew, Cantonese, Hakka and Hainanese — each having its own unique cultural pattern. The Indians also were sharply divided by area of origin, language, religion and customs. They came from India, Sri Lanka, Pakistan and Nepal. Some were Hindu, some Muslim, and the different nationalities kept apart using different worship centres. The Malays were the most homogeneous, but even they originated from different immigrant stock, such as Javanese, Buginese, Batak and Minang. The populace was further fractionalized according to the language medium of education — English, Mandarin, Tamil or Malay. These racial, religious, cultural and linguistic cleavages were a constant source of tension which from time to time erupted into violence. There seemed little hope of building out of such diversity a national identity and a harmonious community.

But Singapore had two assets: competent, visionary leadership and a determined, hard working people (though Koyama's 16 hour working day is somewhat exaggerated). These human resources were the trump card to her survival as an independent nation. Singapore has demonstrated to the world that she is indeed viable. In just over 20 years she has blotted out one of the most densely populated slums in the world and, in a massive urban renewal programme, has relocated 75 per cent of her 2.5 million people in modern, high rise, public housing estates. In the midst of the general economic gloom of the past decade, Singapore boasted full and stable employment, low inflation, a $1.4 billion balance of payments surplus, crime free streets and a government and civil service clean of corruption.

In all of Asia her per capita income is exceeded only by Japan. She has joined the ranks of the developed nations. Multinational companies have flocked to develop bases on her soil. Shenton Way has become a major international financial centre, the port of Singapore ranks as the second busiest in the world, after Rotterdam. Having no oil of her own, she has yet developed a large refining and oil technology industry serving neighbouring countries.

Industry, vision, careful planning and a somewhat autocratic but highly appreciated government has transformed this small nation, teetering on the brink of disaster, into a global city, proud, strong and unified. This mini super-state is a global city because her horizons are global, the world is her hinterland, the ships of every land do business in her waters, her national airline and telecommunications have a worldwide network, her technology and skills are drawn from many nations. And that all this has been done in a city is truly amazing, for as the Deputy Prime Minister Rajaratnam points out,

> By and large men have made a mess of their cities. They have yet to learn how to cope with cities. In the West and more so in Asia most cities are unpleasant places to live in. Many of them are dirty, crime-ridden, anarchic and often violence prone (1976:18).

Donald McGavran observes that the churches have not done well in most of the cities of the world, especially in the cities of the undeveloped or developing world. The great People Movements have taken place among country people (1980:316). Singapore is, in this and many ways, a remarkable urban exception. A People Movement is a significant turning to Christ among a people who share a common race, culture and social class. There is a People Movement daily gaining momentum in Singapore, one that has caused the church to grow from somewhere between 1 and 3 per cent of the population in 1959 to over 11 per cent today. It is that phenomenon which is to become the focus of this study.

In the balance of this chapter we lay out the theoretical basis for our study. As this section is necessarily rather more technical in nature, we would suggest that the more casual reader proceed directly to chapter 2.

## Church Growth in Singapore

Just as most biblical images for the church imply life, so they also suggest growth or reproduction. It is of the nature of the church to grow and multiply itself, just as God's plan has always involved the charge, "be fruitful and multiply" (Gen. 1:28). To this life principle is added the urgency of the Great Commission (Snyder 1977:100).

The mission of the church is to be party with God in the reconciliation of the world to Himself (Col. 1:16-20), to spread the rule of Christ throughout the world, a rule that will be manifest by people joining together as church in worship, fellowship and mission. It is also as church that Christians will fulfil the evangelistic mandate, and as church that reconciliation to God will be demonstrated in a gathered oneness or brotherhood. Kingdom growth will be seen both in the numerical and in the spiritual growth of the church.

This study is given over to observing and analysing the development of the Kingdom as manifest in the growth of the church in Singapore. There is a growing science devoted to such study, a science developed by the Church Growth Movement. The formal definition of the purpose of the Church Growth Movement is set down in the Constitution of the Academy for American Church Growth. It gives us a concise description of the capacity and purpose of this new science which we shall be utilizing in our study of church growth in Singapore.

> Church growth is that science which investigates the planting, multiplication, function and health of Christian churches as they relate specifically to the effective implementation of God's commission to "make disciples of all nations" (Mt. 28:14-20, RSV).
>
> Church growth strives to combine the eternal theological principles of God's Word concerning the expansion of the church with the best insights of contemporary social and behavioral sciences, employing as its initial frame of reference, the foundational work done by Donald McGavran (Wagner 1981a:75).

The growth of the church is ultimately a spiritual phenomenon, the regenerating and renewing work of the Holy Spirit. However, the Spirit works in and through the physical and psychological factors which constitute the context and life of the church.

Sometimes those factors are conducive to growth, sometimes they are not. Sometimes the context is such as to stimulate spiritual hunger and a turning to Christ. Further, pastors by their programmes can provide channels through which the Spirit flows, or they can inadvertently erect barriers which inhibit growth. Church growth pioneer Peter Wagner is in no doubt as to the primacy of the Holy Spirit nor of the essential nature of strategy.

> Ultimately, it is true: the Holy Spirit is the controlling factor in missionary work and the glory for results goes to Him. But .... God has chosen to use human beings to accomplish His evangelistic purposes in the world. These human beings ... may well become obstacles to the work of the Holy Spirit, just as they may well be effective instruments in God's hands.
> Missionary strategy is never intended to be a substitute for the Holy Spirit. Proper strategy is Spirit-inspired and Spirit-governed. Rather than competing with the Holy Spirit, strategy is to be used by the Holy Spirit. ... To set them over against the Holy Spirit is improper, and detrimental to the Lord's work (1971:15).

People will be best discipled (converted and incorporated into the church) and perfected (nurtured) when there is a clear understanding of and sensitivity to church growth factors. Phenomena which facilitate or frustrate church growth we will call church growth "factors" or the "dynamics" of church growth.

There is no one pattern for church growth. The Church Growth Movement presents no preset methods. Each church is unique, and the context in which each is placed is characterized by elements that are not duplicated anywhere else. Donald McGavran warns us against any custom built fix for growth, "for growth occurs in connection with many factors, and these combine and recombine in various parts of the world in almost astronomical variety" (1980:8).

The shaping of strategies and programmes for a church should be based upon a knowledge of the church growth factors that bear on that church's particular situation. Unless they are tailor made they will be less helpful than they could be and may even be quite damaging. A strategy that facilitates rapid growth in one setting might prove a destructive tactic when applied in another context. In fact, because situations are continually changing, assessment of growth factors must also be in a state of perennial revision and strategies must continually be adapted and modified.

The Lord's servants are pilgrims who must never settle into a methodological rut. Our message and goal is set by Scripture and forever remains the same, but in our choice of methods, we must be flexible and sensitive to the situation if the harvest is to be maximized and the spiritual health of the body maintained.

## Purpose and Scope of this Book

Our aim is to identify those growth factors which are significant for the church in Singapore, in order that they may be used by church leaders as a basis for developing strategies and programmes that will increase the harvest. Growth factors may be positive stimuli or negative retardants; it is as important to perceive the traps as it is to recognize the triggers to growth.

One of the working principles of Lyle Schaller's church consulting programme is that people have a great capacity to overcome obstacles, to solve problems and to change conditions. But very often they need help in diagnosing the situation (1978:18). Being generally in accord with this view, I have majored on diagnosis rather than prescription.

While the approach taken in this study is largely macro or city-wide and the growth factors discussed are relevant to most churches, I have, nevertheless, focused attention largely on the Protestant, English-speaking churches which are predominantly Chinese. Only passing reference is made to the vernacular-speaking congregations and to the Roman Catholic Church.

It is among the English-educated Chinese that Christianity is growing so rapidly. This is a large and significant segment of the population, the values and lifestyle of which are increasingly becoming those of the rest of society, due to the government's heavy socialization policy which we will discuss in chapter 4.

However, in spite of this racial and cultural bias, many of the principles discussed have much wider application than to English-speaking Chinese churches. It is hoped, therefore, that this study will benefit other churches as well.

We will follow the system of categorizing growth used by Dean

Hoge and David Roozen in *Understanding Church Growth and Decline; 1950-1978*. Their division of church growth factors into four categories is becoming a standard classification in the Church Growth Movement.

*Contextual factors* are forces operating external to the church and influencing it. They are the backdrop against which the life of the church should be seen. They need to be studied at both national and local levels. *National contextual* factors include the socio-structural, economic, political and value commitments of the community. They also include the physical environment. *Local contextual* phenomena are the immediate neighbourhood influences which bear upon the church and its mission.

*Institutional factors* are the forces of church growth internal to the church itself. *National institutional* factors are seen at the denominational and ecumenical level and include denominational structure, polity, theological orientation, new church development and mission emphases. *Local institutional* factors are most important influences on overall laity satisfaction and include forces internal to the local congregation, such as worship, teaching, leadership, pastoral care and laity mobilization (1979:94-96; 186-197; 321-338).

Hoge and Roozen are convinced that *contextual* factors are of greater significance than institutional factors. Dean Kelley, in his book *Why Conservative Churches are Growing*, sees *national* institutional influences as of paramount importance. Peter Wagner tends to place more emphasis on the functioning of the *local* church (Hoge and Roozen 1979:193-195; 334-343). Probably the varying emphases taken by scholars depends a good deal upon their own perspectives, purposes and range of experience. I would also suggest that the relative importance of these four categories will vary from locus to locus and from time to time. In Singapore it is clearly evident that national contextual factors have been very powerful in recent years, though increasingly institutional factors are becoming of greater import in reaping and preserving the harvest.

The Hoge and Roozen classification is a useful tool, but life is too complex and its many facets too interrelated to fit tidily into any rigid system of categorization. The difficulty in making precise divisions is further compounded when studying a small city-state like Singapore with its all pervading bureaucracy, and when the local context of one public housing estate is almost a mirror of the next. The local and national contexts largely merge. The institutional division also shows an inequality of emphasis because, as we shall see later, local churches tend to be very independent and denominational distinctives muted in Singapore. This means that local congregational factors are correspondingly more determinative than national institutional factors for church growth.

We aim to introduce the reader to as many tools for unearthing growth factors as possible. While the study divides into three parts — contextual factors, institutional factors and strategy — there will inevitably be some overlap. Institutional factors will unexpectedly and inescapably appear in the contextual section and vice versa. For instance, leadership has considerable cultural, contextual input, but it is also influenced by denominational policy, the wishes of the congregation and the personality and ability of the pastor.

Under *contextual* we look first, in chapter 2, at the church in its historical context. Then, in chapter 3, we take an anthropological view of the influence upon the church of traditional Chinese culture and religion. The following chapters, 4, 5 and 6, present a broad spectrum sociological overview of the impact of the ambitious policies of the national government on society and church growth. Chapter 7 then gathers and evaluates relevant Singapore statistical material in search of church growth meaning.

*Institutional* forces will be seen primarily in chapters 8 through 12. Chapter 8 is mostly national institutional, looking at city-wide churchly structures and their influence on growth. In chapters 9 and 10 we come right down to specific things church leaders can do within their congregations to spark growth. Chapter 11 gives attention to three nationwide growth retardants at the congregational level and proffers solutions to these problems. Finally, in chapter 12 some suggestions are made as to a strategy for extension and bridging growth which I see as the way the church should go in order to capitalize on the city's potential for church growth.

## Resources

By virtue of her compact, pluralistic nature, and the ambitious programmes of her government, Singapore is a veritable social laboratory. Its religious and social developments are observed and written up by anthropologists, sociologists, and city planners both in Singapore and from all around the world.

The National Census, taken in June 1980, yielded 1300 pages of raw data which has provided further valuable insights and is especially helpful from our own point of view because, for the first time, religious phenomena were surveyed.

Another source of information was a church growth survey I conducted in 1982. It was primarily a detailed study of 12 congregations, but also included a survey of denominational statistics and reports. The churches studied were selected so as to reflect, as nearly as possible, the true spread of English-speaking churches in the city. Denominationally, there were two each of Brethren Assemblies, Anglican and Assemblies of God and one each of Methodist, Presbyterian, Baptist, Evangelical Free, Christian Nationals Evangelism Commission (CNEC) and Bible Presbyterian. As to age, two of the churches were less than 10 years old, seven came in the 11-30 year bracket and 3 were founded in the previous century or early this century. Three of the churches studied were charismatic, one had a touch and others were non or anti-charismatic. Believing that one may learn both from innovation and non-innovation, success and failure, a few slower growing churches were included in this sample. Two churches had a Decadal Growth Rate (DGR) of over 1,000 per cent. For five, the DGR ranged between 100 and 400 per cent; four had a rate of between 51 and 100 per cent, which for Singapore is rather slow, and one could muster only 27 per cent. The 3,500 questionnaires returned yielded around 140,000 pieces of data which provided valuable insights into both the quantitative and the qualitative aspects of church growth. For subsequent reference this research will be designated *Twelve Churches Study*.

We now turn to the historical development of Singapore in search of factors that have contributed to the growth of the modern church.

## For discussion

1. Compared with other churches in your area, do you rate the growth of your church as fast, moderate or slow? Can you identify any reasons for its growth or lack of growth?
2. What particular type of people is your church reaching? Analyze this from the point of view of race, language, class, and occupational groupings. Are there pockets of other sorts of people in the area who ought also to be the responsibility of your church?

# PART I

## Contextual Factors Influencing Church Growth

# Chapter 2

# Historical Developments: Their Contribution to Church Growth

It was the traders who brought the main religions to Malaya and Singapore. Indian traders introduced Buddhism and Hindusim to Northern Malaya some time in the 4th century after Christ. In the 8th or 9th century Arabs from the Middle East brought Islam to Malaya and Indonesia. Unlike the Europeans of a later era, they integrated with the local people, learning the language and intermarrying, with the result that Islam spread naturally and quickly at the grassroots level. When the Catholic Portuguese traders arrived in the 16th century, Islam was already deeply entrenched throughout Malaya with sultanate rule established as a theocratic government.

In 1511, the Portuguese made Malacca, just over 100 miles from Singapore, their stronghold. The Dutch Protestants, also hungry for control of the East Indies trade, successfully ousted the Portuguese from Java and Malaya in 1641. It was not until 1795 that the British, eyes set on the same lucrative business, reached out from their Indian bases to seize Malacca from the Dutch.

Sir Stamford Raffles, Governor of Bencoolen, set out from India to look for a further base to counter Dutch control of the Straits of Malacca. He landed in Singapore on 29 January 1819 and the following week signed treaties with the Temenggong of Johor and Sultan Hussein, the two absentee landlords of the territory, a treaty which gave the British the right to establish a base on this strategic island with its deep, natural harbour. Penang, Malacca and Singapore together formed the Straits Settlements and were administered by the East India Company until 1867 when the Colonial office in London assumed their control.

After the Japanese occupation of World War II, Singapore became a separate crown colony. A local Legislative Council was set up and Singapore was granted full statehood in December 1959 (Ministry of Culture 1982:172-178).

A full record of the historical development of the church is ably given by Bobby Sng, General Secretary of the Fellowship of Evangelical Students, in the book *In His Good Time: The Story of the Church in Singapore 1819-1978* (1980b). I propose here to survey the history of Singapore in three periods, noting briefly those factors which have been significant to the growth of the church.

## Slow Beginnings for Christianity: 1819-1930

The several hundred years of rule by Christian nations impacted the local populace of the Straits Settlements very little. Why did Christianity fail to spread when Islam, by contrast, was able to make such a total penetration among the indigenous Malays? Seven major contextual reasons for this failure may be discerned.

### Gunboat Diplomacy

The Arab traders came peacefully and mingled freely with the local people and, as they socialized, passed on their religion. By comparison the Portuguese arrived in men-o'-war with crosses on their sails and cannons on their decks, and when Alfonso d'Albuquerque stormed Malacca, he commanded his men to fight bravely to quench the fire of the sect of Mahomet. Their brutal persecution of the Malays built a deep and lasting resentment, and their own nominal Christianity bore a very poor testimony to the Faith. On his visit to the colony, the famous Catholic missionary Francis Xavier was shocked at the immorality and infidelity of the Portuguese and Eurasians, but, like his predecessors, he too had a deep contempt for the Muslims and made no attempt to evangelize them (Wong 1973:25-26).

When the Dutch drove out the Portuguese, they persecuted the remaining Catholics, taking over many of their churches for Protestant chapels or for secular purposes. They too showed scant concern for evangelizing the local people. Not surprisingly, the Straits Chinese (Babas) from Malacca, some of whom migrated to form a significant segment of the Singapore population, have been very resistant to the gospel until very recent times.

The real beginnings of pioneer Protestant work were carried out by the London Missionary Society (LMS), after the coming of the British, in Malacca and in Singapore.

## The Foreign Element

When Raffles founded Singapore in 1819, the island was populated by about 150 Malays, but four months later Raffles wrote that 5,000 people had been added to the thriving colony. By 1824, the population was 10,683 — 3,317 Chinese, 4,580 Malays, 74 Europeans and an assortment of others (Sng 1980b:21).

Despite Raffles' very positive attitude toward Christianity and missionaries, Christianity did not penetrate the Malay/Chinese population. Most Christian energy was spent on the small community of expatriates. The two main churches were the Anglican Cathedral (1838) and the Orchard Road Scotts Church (1872) which were specifically for the expatriate community, very social in nature, and in early days, poorly served by the chaplains of passing ships. By 1892 there were only 140 communicants on the Anglican records. The first Anglican ordination did not take place until 1918, one hundred years after the founding of the Church. The Methodists, beginning in the 1880s, registered 212 members by 1905. The Presbyterians, beginning in 1843, had only 275 members by 1902.

For the most part the churches were neither indigenous nor independent. Even today the Anglicans and Lutherans are heavily dependent on foreign staff, and the Prinsep Street Presbyterian Church, founded in 1843, assumed the full support of its minister only in 1977, and even then, he was still an expatriate.

This failure to concentrate on the local people and to indigenize the ministry is certainly one of the major reasons why the early growth of the Singapore church was so slow. After 100 years only a fraction of one per cent of the population were Christian. There were a few noble souls who had a burden for the Chinese and Malays, but they were few and the long term results of their work rather meagre considering the effort expended. Rev. Fraser and immigrant Tan See Boo worked diligently among the Chinese but, despite fluency in dialect, they had only eleven converts after three years. And early Anglican attempts to evangelize the Tamil Indians were also distressingly slow.

Perhaps the most outstanding missionary was Benjamin Keasberry of the LMS who began a work amongst Malays in 1839. By 1843 60 Malays were attending. He began a boarding school for Malay boys, compiled a Malay hymnal and wrote Christian literature in Malay. He also reached out to the Malay-speaking Babas and began a church for the Chinese in Bukit Timah. When redesignated by the LMS to China, he resigned from his mission in order to continue this work. Keasberry was a man with a real gospel message and a strong pioneer spirit.

However, in 1875 he collapsed and died while preaching, and his work largely died with him. The Malays all reverted to Islam, and there has never since been any significant Malay work in Singapore. The Babas mostly reverted to their former religion leaving a congregation of only 16. By 1902 there were still only 38 members in the Prinsep Street Church and they were little concerned with evangelism.

While Keasberry's work failed, it did indicate that the local people were not totally unreceptive. The failure of his work was due to two particular institutional factors: poor delegation and a social gospel introduced by his successors. Keasberry was a strong, able man with a gospel message, but he failed to train others and could not bring himself to delegate responsibilities to others. This was a major flaw in his ministry that led to its eventual collapse. The leadership of the remnant of the church fell into the hands of people who were more concerned with community service than evangelism. Church growth experts have repeatedly found that churches grow best when there is laity mobilization, a clear evangelistic emphasis, and an evangelical theology (Roof et al. 1979:202-203).

We return now to consider the other powerful contextual forces that inhibited early church growth.

## Temporary Immigrants

It was poverty that prompted most of the Chinese to migrate in search of wealth. After achieving their goal, they intended to return home. They came to Singapore in large numbers hoping to make fortunes by trading or in the newly developed industries of rubber and tin. By 1896, 200,000 a year were arriving in Singapore either to stay or en route to Malaya or Indonesia. They were poor young males and despised merchants of low status.

The Indian immigrants were similarly poverty-stricken and temporary, many being indentured labour. There could hardly be a greater force to hinder such people from converting than the expectation of returning to their native places and their traditional religious systems. As temporary residents, they were not prepared to make permanent, major religious changes.

## Social Scourges

It was the desperate poor who migrated to Singapore. Typically they were young men, too impoverished to rent individual housing and planning only a temporary stay. So they roomed with relatives or anyone who would have them. As the density of population in the built up areas increased, rooms were divided into tiny cubicles for subletting. These were generally unlit, lacked water or toilet facilities and were served by inadequate communal kitchens. Beggars and scavengers, dirt and disease added to the misery of these crowded conditions.

Fully one quarter of the people sought relief in opium and

became addicts. It is a sad fact that in 1910 the colonial government made one third of its income out of opium sales.

The ratio of males to females in 1860 was 14 to 1. In 1870,
80 per cent of the girls in Singapore were prostitutes. The
Manchu dynasty officially forbad females to leave China, thus
aggravating the problem, though merchants managed to smuggle
girls out with the promise of good jobs only to turn them into
prostitutes or, not infrequently, to sell them off to the pirates
who further preyed upon the local people. Only in 1927 were
restrictions put on the importing of prostitutes and not until
the late 1970s did the ratio of male to female begin to approach
parity.

To add to all this, the British used Singapore as a dumping
ground for convicts from other colonies. This small island truly
harboured the dregs of humanity in those early days.

It is not surprising that in such a context secret societies
flourished. These were originally similar to trade unions established for the protection of poor, low paid labour. But, in the
desperation of the situation, they degenerated into terrorist gangs
which thrived on extortion, kidnapping and gambling. In the
1870s, 60 per cent of the people were members of secret societies
while the other 40 per cent were their victims.

Even as late as 1947 more than half the population still lived
in cubicles with no water nor sanitation, and in 1957 a study
revealed that the 4 square miles of the inner city housed 130,000
persons per square mile in single to three storey terraced houses
(Hassan 1970:11). In comparison, the poorest, most heavily
populated area of Los Angeles has a density of 19,000 per
square mile and that in high rise apartments.

These squalid conditions bred a sense of hopelessness that
left people unprepared for religious change. In such rabbit-warren
housing people were difficult to find and still more difficult to
follow up because the population was so mobile. The existing
churches of Chinese and Indians were made up of the poor and
had no resources to give any physical help to the needy. The
secret societies were quick to wreak revenge on any member
who converted. The vicious grip of these societies posed a great
obstacle to the spread of the gospel. Members resigned on pain

of death. In fact, in 1851, after a wave of conversions, there was a savage slaughter of Christians (Sng 1980b:57-59).

In such a society, though many people were attracted to the Christian way, the cost for most was too high in terms of morality, opium, gambling and personal security.

## The Dialect Problem

The multiplicity of languages has retarded the growth of the church from the beginning until today. There are five major Chinese dialects spoken in Singapore plus English, Malay and several Indian languages. This fragmentation makes missionary endeavour very difficult and impedes the flow of the gospel between people. Nowhere in China was there such a cacophony of tongues in such a small area. Even when churches were established, there could be little combined effort to reach the populace with the gospel.

## The Opium War Exodus

In 1838 the Manchu dynasty took action to put an end to the opium trade. The British, their lucrative interests threatened, attacked Chinese ports and the Manchus were soon forced to surrender (1842). Because of British control, China was now open to missionaries and most societies with workers in Singapore quickly withdrew them for, redeployment in China. This greatly set back the Christian cause in Singapore.

In later times many missions simply used Singapore as a stepping stone to China. New workers came for a short time while awaiting an opportunity to enter China. Further, missions were all directed from western home countries and there was often little sensitivity to the needs and opportunities of the local situation.

## The 1929 Depression

A further major setback to church growth was caused by the Depression. Singapore was quite poor, and the Depression hit her very hard. The price of tin and rubber collapsed, businesses failed and many people with no work and no land to farm returned to their homelands. From 1931-1933 emigration exceeded immigration. The numbers returning to their homelands were so great that Anglican Priest Dong Bing Seng (a clergyman who fled China at the Boxer Rebellion), reported a drop in church attendance of more than 50 per cent. This was a tragic blow for the already weak church.

But not all was gloom in the first century of the church in Singapore. By 1900 things were beginning to happen that prepared the way for brighter times.

## Seeds of Hope: 1900-1950

### Christian Immigrants

Among the thousands of Chinese and Indians who migrated in an attempt to escape the unending poverty, unemployment, floods and famines of their own lands, were some Christians. They came in a continual trickle from earliest times, provided a mature leadership base for the young church in Singapore and were a stimulus to numerical growth.

The Indian immigrants mostly came from South India, many from pockets of Christians such as the Tranquebar Mission area originally evangelized by German pietists Ziegenbalg and Pluteschau, others from the Mar Thoma Syrian Church and from Dutch founded churches in Ceylon. The Catholics received the largest number originating from around the ancient Portuguese colony of Goa.

Each of these groups were able to send home for pastors as and when they were needed. This too provided experienced leadership for the church though it did have the negative aspect of fostering an attitude of dependence on the homeland. The result of this was that churches tended to be little replicas of an old tradition in China or India instead of being a contextually relevant model in their new homeland. It also resulted in a failure to develop any pastor training centres in Singapore and Malaysia until the 1950s.

*Refugees from the Boxer Rebellion.* Deep resentment against foreign influence in China led to the Boxer Rebellion (1899 & 1900). Foreigners and Chinese Christians suffered terribly. In all, 135 Protestant and 47 Catholic missionaries were killed and more than 30,000 national believers slaughtered.

Chinese Christians, including pastors and Bible women, fled the violence. A number left in groups with the deliberate intent of forming Christian colonies. Malaya and Singapore received many of these refugees who created witnessing communities among different dialect groups, and so strengthened the church considerably.

## The Immigration Restriction Ordinance

This act, passed in 1930, operated to reduce immigration in three years from 242,000 to 28,000 per annum. The ordinance limited the number of males who could enter but allowed free access to females. It served to stabilize the population. The imbalance between sexes started a process of correction. People began to settle, raise families and think of themselves in terms of Singapore rather than of China or India (Sng 1980b:244). This brought about two contextual conditions significant for the church. First, there was more openness to change due to freedom from traditional ties and a changing mentality. This was reflected in a marked upsurge in church growth.

Second, it caused the baby boom which has constituted the remarkable harvest field of the last 30 years. In 1901 only 11.8 per cent of the population was aged between 5 and 14 years, but in 1957 some 42 per cent was below 14 years of age. These young people are the first major segment of the population to be born and bred as Singaporeans, who "think Singapore" and feel free of the old traditions that prohibited their forebears from becoming Christians.

## John Sung

Any discussion of the movement of people from China in the context of church growth must mention evangelist John Sung. This remarkable man visited Singapore seven times in 1935 and 1936, working through the network of links between churches in China and those in Singapore. No person has made a greater spiritual impact on the city than Sung in those brief, few-day visits. He not only won thousands to Christ but, more significantly, he organized the converts into witness bands of three and sent them out into the streets, and he effectively challenged

Christians to win the lost world to Christ. In his first visit alone there were 1,300 converts, and 111 evangelistic teams incorporating over 500 people were organized. He was no theologian, had many strange ideas and unusual mannerisms, and he irritated the orthodox (Lyall 1961:146-166). Yet throughout Singapore today one finds key Christian leaders and influential lay people who attribute not only their conversion but their model of devotion and commitment to service to the ministry of John Sung.

## Mission Schools

From the very first year of the colony missions were involved in Christian schools. In 1819 Raffles gave permission to Milne of the LMS to start a school for Chinese and Malay boys. Raffles Institute for boys was formed in 1834 and Raffles Girls' School in 1844. In 1886 the Methodists entered the educational arena with the Catholics and Anglicans, followed later by the Presbyterians. For many years the churches were the main bodies bringing education to the people. Their role in education was strongly supported by the government which needed a supply of clerks.

There is no doubt that the Christian schools have served to break down a strong prejudice against Christianity, especially among the Babas. But their impact on church growth is much debated and rather hard to verify positively. When one considers that the Methodists, between 1900 and 1940, had 90 per cent of their missionaries and local ordained staff involved in the schools, and the bulk of their funds tied up in this ministry, one cannot but question the strategy. Certainly in the 1930-1950 period, when most teachers were either liberals or lacked spiritual dedication, the schools had very little evangelistic impact. One other thing is noteworthy: mission schools were almost entirely English medium, and this has meant that the Chinese speaking churches lacked local educated leadership. We will discuss mission schools further in chapter 8.

So while the seeds of hope were planted in the first half of the century and there was some growth, it was not until the early 1950s that the harvest began in earnest. We touch only briefly on it here because its tremendous significance will be developed more fully in chapters 5, 6 and 7.

## Harvest Time: 1950s — 1980s

A number of factors coincided with the baby boom of the 1950s to the 1970s to stimulate the extraordinary church growth that has taken place. Some of these things are at least in part institutional growth factors, nevertheless they are best dealt with here.

### British Heritage and Western Orientation

In many postcolonial countries there is a residue of antiwestern feeling, but this is not true of Singapore. When in 1971 the British decided they could no longer maintain a presence in Singapore, there were loud laments and much sadness, even fear for the future. Singapore very definitely and proudly follows a British tradition: in its parliamentary model, legal system, marriage law and customs, education system, and so on. British university degrees are preferred to local degrees and even to degrees from such prestigious universities as Tokyo and Harvard, while students still study Dickens and Shakespeare (Wu 1975:1-2). While this is true, Singapore feels neither inferior to nor indebted to Britain.

The significant effect of this strange anomaly is that modern Singaporeans, in spite of their loudly-acclaimed and tourist-promoted Asian distinctives, are more oriented to western than to eastern traditions. Consequently Christianity, coming to Singapore as it does primarily from western sources, is also viewed more positively.

The colonial government followed a policy of segregating the races into different residental areas and even to some degree, stratifying them occupationally (Hassan 1970:9-14). Since the deaths and injuries in the 1964 racial riots, the national government has, with added determination, worked toward racial integration and harmony. The new public housing was desegregated and English was encouraged both to create a common medium of communication between citizens and also as a link with the outside world which was to be the source of Singapore's technology and future prosperity. This new policy made young people even more open to western ideas. Christianity also, with its English literature, agencies and missionaries from the West, has taken on a new degree of acceptability.

## Independent Nationhood and Urban Renewal

With the coming of World War II and the Japanese occupation, the supply of pastors from China and India dried up and foreign missionary staff were repatriated. The churches of Singapore and Malaya began to realize they had to stand on their own feet and there developed, both in the church and in society, a new spirit of independence. After the War, Singapore quickly moved toward self-government which further served to underline to the church that she must care for herself. The fruit of this contextual change can be seen in the founding of the first two national seminaries: Trinity Theological College (1948) and Singapore Bible College (1952).

It was on 9 August 1965 that Singapore suddenly found herself cut off from Malaysia and forced to go it alone as a nation. Though a shock to Singaporeans at every level, the change had unrealized advantages for the Singapore church. Much of the church's finance and leadership had previously been drained off to help weaker works in East and West Malaysia. Now that it was no longer a feeder station for the much larger Federation, manpower and funds were released and attention focused on the breathtaking harvesting opportunities in Singapore itself. Gradually denominations and missions began to recognize and administer Malaysia and Singapore as two separate fields, synods, conferences or associations. Singapore became a mission field in its own right. The political division therefore proved to be a significant contextual stimulus to church growth.

At the same time, the new national government (1960) embarked on a course that would completely change society. It set out to upgrade the nation's housing, to industrialize, to modernize education, to bring about radical integration and to establish a national identity. This will be the central subject of chapters 4, 5 and 6. It is sufficient to say here that this pushed Singaporeans into a lifestyle characterized by constant and radical change. It also made them a people oriented to the future rather than to the past.

Their traditional religion is part of the past. Christianity is being associated with the future, part of the new and, supposedly, better world.

## New Missionaries, Churches and Christian Agencies

In 1949 a flood of missionaries began to exit from Communist China and to look for new fields of service among Chinese people. Some of these veterans came to Singapore and fulfilled a pivotal function. They ministered in the dialect churches which were becoming rather ingrown and in need of fresh challenge. They also staffed or guided many of the new English-speaking congregations that were just springing up; congregations composed of the new generation youth. They often functioned as something of a bridge between the old and the new. The providence of God is certainly seen in this infusion of a trained and sensitive labour force open to both the old traditions of China and to the new ways of the West.

Due to a number of factors, not the least being this vast exodus of workers from China, and the rising tide of missions in America, the 1950s saw a new convergence of missionary and evangelistic bodies on Singapore. It was these newly arriving bodies that provided fresh zeal and capacity for evangelizing the masses of receptive young people. In 1950-1964 the big four denominations in Singapore — Anglicans, Methodists, Brethren and Presbyterian — planted 20 new works. However, even more startling was the fact that four new denominations on the Singapore scene in the 1950s — the Southern Baptists, Lutheran Church of America, Christian Nationals Evangelism Commission (CNEC) and the Bible Presbyterians — were able, in the same period, to commence work and establish 22 new congregations. Other newcomers were the Assemblies of God, the Seventh Day Adventists and the Evangelical Free Church, all of which had little trouble getting established.

The parachurch organizations also arrived and made an immediate impact, especially among the English speaking young people. These included the Overseas Missionary Fellowship (OMF, 1952), the Varsity Christian Fellowship (VCF, 1952), Youth for Christ (YFC, 1956), the Scripture Union and Inter

School Christian Fellowship (ISCF, 1958), the Navigators and later Campus Crusades for Christ (CCC) and Teen Challenge. The degree of receptivity, the causes of which we will further analyse in chapters 4, 5 and 6, and the dimensions of the harvesting are indicated by some statistics which were gathered by Bobby Sng. During the first ten years of its ministry, YFC and ISCF together registered 10,000 decisions for Christ and by the mid-1960s they were together reaching about 2,500 students per week in their regular student groups (Sng 1980b:246-248).

Clearly it was in the providence of God that this striking number of largely foreign, English medium, evangelistic agencies should move into Singapore just at the time when Singapore's baby boom began to enter the teen years, a generation of youngsters educated in English and reaching out to embrace the new world that Independence and modernization were offering them. Unprecedented receptivity was matched by unparallelled capacity to harvest.

## The Communist Threat

Since 1948 the threat of Communism has ever hung over Malaysia and Singapore, giving to the church and to society generally a sense of the possible shortness of time. From 1948 to 1960 Malaya and Singapore were living under a declared state of emergency as they fought the Malayan Communist Party in the jungles. No sooner was that crisis averted than Singapore's southern neighbour Indonesia appeared to be moving rapidly into the Communist camp. With the nearest Indonesian islands located only two miles off the Singapore coast, the threat was real and immediate and fear was rife. After the abortive coup d'etat in Indonesia came the crisis in Indochina. The consequent fall of Vietnam, Laos and Cambodia added to the sense of urgency in the church and increased the feeling of insecurity and uncertainty among the populace at large. Such insecurity increases receptivity.

The final two items to be discussed here are strictly institutional phenomena but they belong to this discussion.

## The Rise of Lay Ministry

With the rapid growth of the Christian church as indicated by the denominational figures already given, and the numerous small independent churches which frequently grew out of school fellowship groups, there was a sudden and serious lack of trained leadership. The growth had outstripped the local supply of trained leaders and with China now Communist and Singapore having strict restrictions on immigration, the church could no longer draw extensively from outside sources for labour. In some ways the quality of ministry and level of strategic activity may have suffered as a result, but the positive benefits have been profound too. The laity have taken positions of leadership and responsibility to a degree found in few places in the free world. The many house churches have been largely planted and run by laity, and this has been so common that there is a widespread confidence among the laity that ministry is part of their responsibility. Laity mobilization is generally recognized to be a central institutional growth factor and it has certainly contributed greatly to the evangelistic impetus of the church in Singapore. I would suggest that the student oriented parachurch organizations have been very significant both in training lay young people and in giving them a sense of responsibility and the right to minister even though unordained.

## The Battle for Truth

From the 1930s many of the denominational missionaries were theologically quite liberal. As in the mission schools, they also had considerable influence in Trinity Theological College. But from the 1950s, the growing national spirit has been reflected in more freedom among national Christians to question and reject this theology. Liberal western missionaries have gradually been replaced by nationals who are, in the main, theologically more conservative. In 1952 Singapore Bible College was founded to provide an evangelical alternative for pastor training, and in 1950, Timothy Tow, influenced by the International Council of Christian Churches (ICCC), broke from the Presbyterian Church to form the new and rapidly growing Bible Presbyterian denomination. By 1971 it had 13 congregations and 828 members, increasing by 1983 to 27 congregations and 4,105 active members. Dean Kelley, in his research on American churches, also discovered that churches which were clear. in their beliefs, strict in their membership requirements, rather isolationist and actively evangelistic, grew much faster than those with a social message, ecumenical associations and easy membership terms (1972:20-31). We seem to have here a fairly universal institutional growth factor.

In summary we can conclude that the powerful contextual forces that operated to retard church growth in the early history of the colony have now given place to a new set of contextual factors which are overwhelmingly conducive to growth.

In the following chapter we shall again step back into history, this time to study the impact of the imported traditional religions on church growth in Singapore.

## For discussion

Consider your own church in relation to its growth. Bearing the following categories in mind, analyze the growth factors. Make two lists: (1) those that are positive stimuli to growth and (2) those that are retardants to growth.

Categories to analyze:  historical development
values of society
housing patterns
education
government policies
church location
church structure/organization
church premises/accommodation

(Preliminary thought in this area will ensure that you receive greater benefit from the study of subsequent chapters.)

# Chapter 3
# The Backdrop:
# Religion and Tradition

To the noisy clanging of gongs and in an atmosphere heavy with the aroma of incense, the spirit medium leapt about, spiked with huge skewers, speaking in tongues and casting lucky coins to the bystanders. I happened on this familiar Chinese ritual while returning from a nearby church which was located in a large public housing estate of modern high-rise apartments. The old persists incongruously alongside the new. And as Marguerite Kraft points out,

> When there is a change in the religious system, the old provides the building blocks for the new. Old religions do not die; they live on in the new religions which follow them (1978:72-73).

When one considers that ten years ago probably in excess of 90 per cent of the population held to some form of traditional non-Christian religion, one cannot but realize that traditional religions are part of the church growth context that must be taken into careful account.

As it is not possible in this study to analyze each of the local religions in detail, I have opted to investigate the mos pervasive, and that is the traditional religion of the Chinese who make up 77 per cent of the population. In the 1980 Census, 73 per cent* of all Chinese still confessed allegiance to their traditional Chinese religion. Further, 79 per cent of Christians were Chinese, and the majority of these were converted in the previous ten years from traditionalist backgrounds and many were still living in homes where the old religious practices continued to be observed. Of the 16 per cent of Chinese who confessed no religion, most had lost faith in their traditional religion sometime over the last ten years. This religious context is a very central and immediate one, and a tradition of 5,000 years cannot be obliterated in one or two generations.

While we cannot study Hindu and Muslim religious traditions here, we may make the fairly safe generalization that the same prevalence of superstition, animistic phenomena and involvement with spirits is evidenced in the Indian and Malay traditional religions as in the Chinese. The folk level of religion is far more important for the vast majority than the philosophical versions of those faiths.

## Chinese Religionists in Singapore

As we saw above, in the 1980 Singapore Census 73 per cent of the Chinese people declared themselves to be Buddhist or Taoist. Almost 11 per cent stated that they were Christians and the remaining 16 per cent declared themselves to have "no religion". These statistics are a little misleading, for of these 1.4 million self-styled Buddhists and Taoists, only about 25,000 are in any way associated with what is technically Buddhism or Taoism.

For the purpose of this study we will call these 1.4 million "Chinese Religionists". Topley calls their beliefs "anonymous religion", Elliot, "Shenism" (gods), and Comber, "religion of the masses". Others have labelled it "folk" or "peasant" religion. Most Chinese Religionists would have preferred to say that their religion was "pai shen" (worship of the gods and spirits), but the statisticians did not give them that alternative.

It has been found that most so-called Buddhists know nothing of the historical person behind the modern Buddha icon (Wee

1977:156), few could state even one of the Four Noble Truths, few understand or believe in the doctrine of "karma" (reaping what one sows), nor could explain the yin-yang concept so foundational to philosophical Chinese religion. In fact, the religion of the Singaporean Chinese Religionist is an ancient, rather animistic folk religion infused, to a small degree, by a selection of often modified beliefs and practices from the so-called high religions in something of the proportions depicted in Figure 1.

CONFUCIANISM

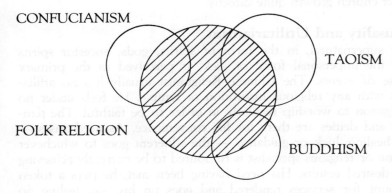

TAOISM

FOLK RELIGION

BUDDHISM

Figure 1. Chinese Religion in Singapore.

In her extensive research, Vivienne Wee has, I believe, rightly concluded that the central tenet of Singapore Chinese Religion is "fate". Fate is an impersonal force. It cannot be modified either by men or gods. Each individual must live out his fate. However, within that fate a person's luck may fluctuate considerably.

The central motivation of Chinese Religion is to discover ways of avoiding trouble when luck is contrary and of gaining the maximum advantage from the fleeting moments when luck is good (Wee 1977:144-160). Gambling, "the great social evil" of Chinese society, is deemed the best way of reaping countable, storable benefits from periods of good luck. People consult astrologers and spirit mediums to discover whether their luck at any given time is good or bad. Having ascertained this, they then go to the gods or ancestor spirits for specific guidance as to what numbers will be lucky for gambling and what things they should do to capitalize on their luck. Almost every one of some 1,000 temples in Singapore have facilities for determining lucky gambling numbers.

We will observe other features of Chinese Religion as we discuss their contextual significance for church growth. I propose to discuss six central aspects of this traditional religion that affect church growth quite directly.

## Causality and Utilitarianism

The supernatural, in the form of spirits, gods, ancestor spirits and the impersonal force of luck, is perceived as the primary cause of events. The Chinese Religionist usually has no affiliation with any religious institution or temple. He feels under no obligation to worship regularly in order to be faithful. The temples and deities are there for his convenience. As need arises — for healing, luck or guidance — the adherent goes to whichever shrine or religious specialist is rumoured to be currently achieving the desired results. His need having been met, he pays a token amount for services rendered and goes on his way feeling no further obligation toward the one that helped him. So, in Singapore, Chinese Religionists are found in Thai Buddhist temples praying to the Buddha, in Hindu temples beseeching luck from the bodhi tree or one of the many Hindu deities, or even in a Catholic church praying to one of the statues and burning joss sticks (Wee 1977:371-382, 424-425).

Even priests, diviners and mediums function as independent individuals, answerable to no one and, at most, loosely affiliated with the recently formed voluntary Buddhist Association. Most of the temples were founded by independent monks or healers and they or their family continue their administration. Monks, temples and deities are all patronized only so long as they are deemed helpful, after which they are neglected; the temples fall into dispair or revert to ordinary homes and the religious functionary takes up another occupation.

Furthermore, deities are not the masters of men. They are finite and may be deceived, manipulated or bribed to fulfil the whims of individual human beings. In this truly anthropocentric system the deities are wholly vulnerable. Many have fallen prey to the process of obsolescence. The traditional gods of politics, scholarship and nature are among those who find no place in the temples of modernizing, urban Singapore (Yang 1961:11-13). For instance, as Singaporeans move into the comparative safety of concrete housing units and the fear of slum fires becomes a thing of the past, so also Huo-shen, the Preventer of Fire, will be relegated to the irrelevant category.

Again, because fate is attached primarily to the individual rather than to the family or business, the Chinese have preferred the small scale, personally controlled business (Wee 1977: 433). The Singapore government has faced a lot of difficulty convincing local Chinese businessmen to put their capital into larger, public manufacturing companies.

Even ancestor worship has a strong egoistic flavour, for if the ancestor spirits are honoured and cared for they will bring good fortune to the family, and from their broader horizons they can be a source of guidance. But should they be neglected, they may become very vengeful and troublesome.

In summary then, Chinese Religion is characterized by five things. First, it is *result oriented and highly pragmatic*. Second, it is *problem oriented*. Most people do not exhibit much religious behaviour unless they anticipate or are experiencing problems (Wee 1977:440).

Third, Chinese religion is very *this-worldly and materialistic* and for two reasons. Fate has it that the destiny of men in the next world is immutable, and so the only hope of gain is to be prosperous in this life. And by heritage the Chinese who migrated from China were mostly poor merchants and poorer peasants, both despised, low status groups. The only way for them to achieve status was to gain wealth and latterly, education, the goose that lays the golden eggs. As a result, Chinese Religion in Singapore has undergone a number of mutations in this direction. Tua Peh Kong, the god of prosperity, a somewhat insignificant deity back in China, has been elevated to eminence in the Lion

City. Gambling related to divine guidance is endemic, and paper replicas of cars, aeroplanes, houses and clothes are ceremonially burned to supply the ancestor with all his needs in the next world which are also perceived of in a very materialistic way.

Fourth, Chinese Religion is very *individualistic*. There is little community outside the Chinese family as we shall shortly see. Religion is not a communal affair. People normally go to the temples as individuals, they worship before the ancestor tablets and deities and leave. Even individual family members often frequent different temples.

Finally, it is a *highly concrete, action based religion*, not at all philosophically oriented. Paul Clasper lists several Chinese characteristics, among which he included the following three:

    a.    Emphasis on the concrete rather than the abstract as the bearer of meaning.

    b.    A vivid sense of the relational, personal and utterly practical .... the Chinese are inherently existential and consistently suspicious of the detached, and the speculative.

    c.    A rhythm which implies action first, then reflection (1977: 12).

When Buddhism came from India, its writings were full of speculation, fantasy and abstract philosophical dialogue. The Chinese translated the more practical sections of these writings, the rest they either ignored or rewrote (Nakamura 1964:185-195). Even the Chinese characters express this love for the concrete and Chinese proverbs such as "a square peg in a round hole", are famous for their lucidity.

These traditional attitudes to religion have significant implications for church growth. Several are suggested here.

***They stress the paramount need for concrete and practical religion.***
In the context of very earthy, practical Chinese Religion, the level of abstraction in the church is quite unpalatable. No religion at any point in the history of Christendom has been so heavily biased toward the cognitive — doctrine and theology — as has Protestantism. Certainly the Bible does not reflect the level of abstraction demonstrated by the church today.

If the Chinese need healing or an evil spirit exorcised, they go to the temple sure of some help. When guidance is required as to the choosing of a career or a marriage partner, the auspicious time to take a holiday, when to have a child or make a business deal, the diviners and spirit mediums will have some practical, concrete guidance to give, and not uncommonly, the guidance proves to be right; the Evil One sees to that. Most church workers in Singapore have no experience of healing, exorcism, words of knowledge or prophecy. They are simply not equipped to minister at that practical level despite the clear Scriptural picture of just such a pattern of Christianity. Some who turn to the Christian way resort to their old sources of help in time of need. Many will not be willing to entrust their lives to Christ until there is evidence that the Spirit of God can help them as the spirits of their traditional deities and ancestors have done in the past. Gail Law, of the Chinese Coordination Centre of World Evangelism (CCCOWE), commenting on Christianity in Chinese Hong Kong, says,

> Generally they have great difficulty in comprehending the concept of absolute value being in God himself. That Christians should commit themselves *entirely* to God is a concept that is too risky to try. To their thinking — which gives money, fame, and pleasure top value — Christianity is *impractical* and therefore unacceptable (1981:93; emphasis added).

The blatant pragmatism of the Chinese is not just characteristic of the older generation. Modern westernizing Singaporeans show this trait as clearly as do their parents. For instance, at the university I saw an official computer printout on the notice board listing not only which degrees, but which combination of subjects, brings the maximum income in the employment field. If the church is to appeal to people from such a background, then the Christianity we present must be practical and life-changing right down at the gut level of healing for the body, daily guidance and answered prayer. Anything less lacks credibility to many.

J. Herbert Kane, a veteran missionary from China and missiologist, said,

> Western thought is concerned with truth and the western mind

is intrigued by reason. Hence our emphasis on logic. We vainly imagine that if we can win the argument, we will win the adversary. The Oriental mind, on the other hand, is not primarily interested in truth, still less in logic. Christian theology has emphasized truth to the neglect of power .... Religion to be viable must be vital as well as valid (1976:309).

This is no new discovery. Long ago Paul said,

When I came to you, brethren, I did not come with superiority of speech or wisdom ... my message and my preaching were not in persuasive words of wisdom, but in *demonstration* of the Spirit and of *power*, that your faith should not rest on the wisdom of men, but on the *power* of God (1 Cor. 2:1-5; emphasis added.)

Evidence from all around the world suggests the greater effectiveness of a practical and power supported ministry than one that is reliant totally on words. Peter Wagner has found that one of the major forces for church growth in Latin America is the free operation of all the gifts of the Spirit, especially healing (1979b:14). Charles Kraft believes that for Africa, if the church does not exercise a ministry of healing and exorcism, Christianity will lack credibility (1979:305).

Yonggi Cho insists that in the heart of man there is placed by God a belief in the miraculous related to the image of the miraculous God within, and unless they see miracles, people will not be convinced that our God is the real God (1979:64). Leslie Lyall, in his biography of John Sung, says that the Chinese have always expected healing from God, and no man is considered a real minister unless he heals. According to Lyall, one of the secrets of Sung's fruitfulness was a significant healing ministry in all his campaigns (1961:132-137). In the book *I Will Build My Church: Ten Case Studies of Church Growth in Taiwan* (Swanson 1978), it is noteworthy that the factor that sparked growth in most of these churches was a case of healing early in the life of the church. Swanson concludes that the Chinese are pragmatists, more interested in what works in their daily lives than in pure dogma and doctrine (1971:76-79).

Church statistics in Singapore also testify clearly to this contextual phenomenon. The fastest growing churches in the city are all charismatic and it is notable that it is those charismatic churches that have a ministry in healing, exorcism and crisis counselling. An older Anglican church, Our Saviour's, is a clear example of the impact of healing and crisis counselling in the Singapore Chinese context. Our Saviour's, founded in 1956, grew to have a Sunday attendance of 120 by 1977. Over the fastest period of its early growth (1971-1977) the DGR was 140 per cent. Derek Hong, a new ordinand and a charismatic, became priest in charge in 1977. With a ministry focused on healing and crisis care the average attendance soared from 120 to 419 over the next four years, which is a DGR of 1,278 per cent. In the religious milieu discussed above, such a ministry, conducted at a very practical level and without neglecting teaching and knowledge, is fundamental to maximizing the harvest.

*They indicate causes for the high number of drop-outs.* Probably the single, most sounded criticism of the church in Singapore is that her converts do not last. The rapid growth of the church indicates that the situation is not as bad as it is often made out to be. However, as this problem of attrition does appear to be acute, we will discuss it in more detail in chapter 11.

The dimensions of the problem can be seen in a few typical figures. In 1971 James Wong calculated that around 43 per cent of Anglicans were inactive (1973:102). Frankel Brethren Assembly, after 25 years of existence in a very stable community, shows an attrition rate of 23 per cent. Grace Baptist, on examination, could not locate 33 per cent of its members, and all of this in a largely first generation church. In my *Twelve Churches Study* I found that 42 per cent of those surveyed had become Christians in the last five years, and only 16 per cent had been Christians more than ten years. Evidently new converts are going out the back door at a considerable rate. Part of the reason for this, I believe, is found in the religious context just discussed.

I have not been able to do a detailed study of the attrition rate in the churches with a healing ministry, but preliminary evidence would suggest that their attrition rate is lower. It would appear that Singaporeans are being attracted by the truth of Christianity but are then being disenchanted by its lack of practical helpfulness. Many churches are far too cerebral in their approach and need to present a Christianity not only strong in truth and promise for the future, but also attractive in terms of strength and help for daily living. Sociologist John Clammer, having studied the Singapore situation, concluded that,

> There is a great lack of emphasis on the social aspects of belief, which tends to give Christianity a negative response in the minds of non-Christians, who often look upon it as a religion of "talking", but not doing (1981:32).

I would suggest that converts to Christianity are making the same disappointing discovery. The church is not exemplifying the practical level of religion and the power of God that is seen in its text book the Bible.

Further, in line with Chinese pragmatism, some embrace Christianity at a time of need and then later, when life is running smoothly again, they drop out for a time: problem oriented religion.

The Chinese are recognized as having a high level of individualism in their culture. Sun Yat Sen likened his own race to a plate of dry sand. The family has traditionally been the only strong centre of communal life, but the generation and linguistic gap that has developed has broken down even that level of community, leaving a society-wide vacuum in "belongingness". Young people are coming to the church hungry for the community or fellowship which it advertises, but often finding that underneath the superficial togetherness, the church is just like the rest of society, a collection of unbonded individuals. If the church is to become a truly caring community, it has a very deep-rooted obstacle to overcome in this inherent Chinese individualism and lack of cohesiveness.

**They show the need for active religious expression.** Not only are the fastest growing churches in Singapore characterized by a practical ministry in healing, exorcism and crisis counselling, but they also fulfil the traditional need for active religion. The Assemblies of God (AOG) churches are a clear illustration of this. The predominant place given to worship and the style of worship adopted is undoubtedly a major reason for their growth. There is a high degree of participation by the worshippers in music, singing, praying aloud, body movements, clapping, hand raising, laying on of hands, hugging and so forth as active expressions

of religious emotion. Such expressions are open and meaningful to everyone regardless of the levels of intellectual ability.
It is noteworthy that the AOG denomination as a whole has
shown a DGR of 635 per cent in the last ten years, while in the
same period no other denomination has a DGR in excess of 300
per cent. Two outstanding examples are Trinity Christian Centre
(AOG) and Calvary Charismatic Fellowship (AOG) which, in
the last six years, have grown from a handful of worshippers
to weekly attendances of 2,000 and 3,300 respectively.

*They suggest reasons for weak church loyalty.* One of the problems
that churches in Singapore face is that of a lack of commitment to the church. In the *Twelve Churches Study* I found that
37 per cent of those attending services were not in membership
at that church. At Grace Baptist 51 per cent of non-members
present were, in practice, regular worshippers at the church! Over
all, 40 per cent of adherents had once been in other churches
though most had been Christians less five years.

In another study, Bobby Sng found that only 66 per cent of
Christian tertiary students had been baptized, and of those un-
baptized it was disconcerting to find that 29 per cent had been
Christians more than five years (1980a:7).

Do we not see reflected here the strong influence of their
traditional religious heritage? Undoubtedly there is a real problem
of lack of commitment to a particular church and this of course
greatly limits the capacity of the churches to build the stable
communities which are socially satisfying and so badly needed.

Some of the young people are not baptized because of parental
objection. But I would suggest that a substantial part of the
problem lies in the Chinese utilitarianism that fails to see any
personal value in such an exercise. Influenced also by parachurch
attitudes, many young people see baptism as no more than a
purely symbolic action.

Many Christians move freely between denominations showing
little concern for theological distinctives — another traditional
emphasis.

Independent churches also mark Chinese society. One study,
by Ho Wing Onn, done as far back as 1959 when denominational missions were still very much to the fore, found that
5,000 of the 40,000 Protestants were in independent churches

Nyce concluded in 1970 that independent churches were then the fastest growing sector of Christianity (1970:42). According to the Singapore Church Directory 1982-1983, 63, or 25 per cent of all congregations listed, were independent congregations (Kao 1982). And one suspects that, if all the unlisted house churches were able to be tabulated, the figure would go even higher. The old Chinese spirit of independence and non-alignment with any particular religious institution is evident again. These things do not make for a cohesive and strong church.

## Diffused Religion

Folk Religion has always been the primary belief system of the Chinese masses. The reason why so little is written about it is that it operates largely unnoticed, diffused throughout the various "secular" institutions of society. For instance, as part of family life ancestors are worshipped and the kitchen god sent on his annual pilgrimage to Heaven by burning his effigy. As part of the village communal life and agriculture the nature gods received their offerings; a community affair. Later, as part of state government ceremonies, Heaven (Tien) was worshipped by the Emperor who was Heaven's representative on earth. Occupational guilds have a patron deity housed in their societal headquarters, and so we could go on. Chinese Religion is almost impossible to separate from the daily secular functions of life. In fact, one might say that nothing is fully secular and nothing totally religious. Confucian moral teachings, to the extent that the masses embraced them, were integrated into that pre-existing system. Taoism and Buddhism, on the other hand, set up their own religious institutions and made religion a separate subsystem that could stand on its own. They stood apart from the family, guilds and government, making themselves an optional area of life. Partly because of this, they have remained the religion of a select elit. The masses simply incorporated a small selection of Taoist and Buddhist features into their already amorphous, diffused religion.

The institutional religions were never popular with the masses, being too philosophical and abstract. Diffused religion, on the other hand, lacked a clearly defined system of beliefs or any trained authorities to explain its meaning and practice. It has been almost entirely a laity movement (Yang 1961:294-340; Hsieh 1978:214-216).

This diffused state of religion has had an impact on Christianity in a number of ways. I will describe six of them here.

First, Singaporeans tend to place little store by the structural, institutional aspects of religion as we have already noted. Commitment to the particular institutional forms of Christianity have been rather weak, but given the aforesaid context, this should not automatically be interpreted as a weak commitment to Christ and to Christianity.

Second, the traditional context should probably be a warning to the church not to structure itself into a heavily bureaucratic system. The church should travel with a minimum of institutional baggage.

Third, there is a strong tradition of lay leadership in religion, a phenomenon already noticeable in Singapore Christianity; and a feature to be encouraged if we desire maximum church growth. The church in Singapore is greatly advantaged in being freer than the West from a sense of dependence upon full time clergy, who are often assumed to be spiritually more effectual.

Fourth, in one study, covering 19 churches, it was found that 25 per cent of Christians were involved in a Christian group related to their place of work (Sng 1980a:10-11). In my *Twelve Churches Study* I discovered that 42 per cent of respondents had been involved in parachurch groups during their student days. When one considers that many Christians went to school before the era of parachurch organizations, this figure is very high. In the same study, where 19.6 per cent of respondents were currently students, 16.8 per cent of all respondents were involved in parachurch groups, indicating a very high level of student involvement in parachurch activities.

If I am not mistaken, these groups are really semidiffused religion. They, like the old Chinese guilds, are part of the social circuit of the Christians of Singapore. It is probably because of the context of diffused religion that they have been so well accepted and become such a very powerful instrument for evangelism and nurture. It is religion out among the people; student and occupational guilds.

The final two points relate to the vulnerability of diffused religion. When the social institution upon which diffused religion depends collapses, then diffused religion dies with it, for it cannot stand on its own. When the Chinese came under the British system of government, religious practices relating to the ruler's mandate from Heaven faded out. When western patterns of commerce prevailed in Singapore, the old occupational guilds began to die, and many artisans lost their religious base. When the goverment stamped out the secret societies because of their involvement in gangsterism, many of the poor of Singapore found a major facet of their religion swept from under their feet. The incursion of western family patterns and values has greatly undermined the religion of the home, including ancestor worship. All these social changes have struck at the roots of Chinese Religion in Singapore, creating a religious vacuum that has probably been the single greatest cause of the growth of Christianity.

Last, the lack of trained religious personnel has meant that when young people question the meaning and validity of traditional religion, there has been no one to give them a credible answer. Joseph Tamney notes that there is virtually no attempt in Singapore to reform traditional religion so as to make it credible to the modern generation (1970a:260). Institutional Buddhism can reform, but without institutions, there is little possibility of arresting the massive exodus from folk religion.

## Kinship and Ancestor Veneration

Lawrence Thompson, speaking of traditional Chinese society, comments,

> The central importance of family is no doubt the specific distinguishing characteristic of Chinese society; and the function of the ancestral cult is certainly the specific distinguishing characteristic of the Chinese family. Family religion is basic, while individual religion is secondary (1969:34).

In traditional Chinese society the family stood out clearly as by far its most powerful institution, the institution which gave shape to the whole of society. Upon it all other lesser institutions were modelled, including government. Bound up in the importance of the family was the belief in reincarnation and the related veneration of ancestors to whom the living resorted for help and guidance. We will begin this section by briefly observing the form and function of these two related institutions.

**Kinship.** The fact that the family was the keystone in the arch of Chinese society is reflected in there being over one hundred terms to designate various family relationships (Swanson 1971:67). In Singapore the church and the government's urban renewal programme have often been forced to shoulder the blame for the break-up of the Chinese family, and the consequent slide in moral standards in society. But that is not fair, because the traditional Chinese family system never did exist in Singapore.

The pattern of migration was such that most people who came to Singapore came as single males who left family, clan land and related customs behind. Even when wives came too, the extended family structure was disrupted. Widespread polygamy along with urban crowding and cubicle living, made even nuclear families difficult to sustain.

In 1957, before urban renewal began, the "one family nucleus" was the norm for 70 per cent of the people. When in 1960 the government began to rehouse the population, it did not break up extended families as is commonly and erroneously supposed, for only the low income people were moved, and it was noticeably the wealthy who could afford to live as extended families (Kuo and Wong 1979b). In fact, the 1970 Census revealed that 71.5 per cent of the total households in Singapore were single nucleus — virtually no change from the previous figure throughout the period when growth in Christianity and industrialization were most marked (Chen and Tai 1977:88). Ray Nyce, in his detailed study, comes to the same conclusion and also quotes a study on Indians to show that the same forces applied to that community too (1970:59-60).

But though the kinship system is quite different from that in China, it is still very significant, constituting for most people the strongest social ties in the city. Among the values it continues to reinforce are male centredness, respect for age, emotional reservedness, dependence, submission, obedience, orientation to the past, conservatism, security, loyalty, filial piety, ancestor veneration and group dominance over the individual. While there is a lot of cohesion and loyalty within the Chinese family, there is very little in the community at large. This means that when family solidarity is eroded, society loses the cohesion, community and moral values that were primarily created and enforced within the family circle.

**Ancestor Veneration.** As the Chinese family is the crux of society, so the family is the orbit around which religion revolves, and ancestor veneration is the centre of that family religion.

The ancestors receive much more attention than the vast pantheon of Chinese gods and goddesses, and even when the gods are consulted, it is invariably with regard to family matters. J.T. Addison, I believe, is correct in seeing "ancestor worship as the most important religious phenomenon in the life of the people" (1925:83). The main Chinese festivals are all family and ancestor centred. What then is the function of ancestor veneration that it should become the central aspect of both social and religious life? There are two major areas of ancestral significance: religious and social.

a) Religious Function. The Chinese family and cosmology are on the same continuum of history which is marked by the reincarnational cycle. Death, far from severing relationships, simply elevates them to a new plane. Paternal authority does not cease at death. Obedience in life is followed by reverence and service after death. There are three major religious values in ancestor worship:

i) Guidance. The ancestor spirit continues to reside in the ancestral tablet in the family home. He can be consulted for advice as to lucky numbers for gambling, the cause of illness and other family related matters.

ii) Mutual care. Life in the spirit is much the same as life in the body. As a spirit one still needs food, clothing, money, transport and so forth. By burning paper models (alchemy) these items are transmuted to the ancestor. Food is offered from which the ancestor extracts the spiritual essence. This system is a method of expression of love and care for the forebear, who also hovers over his living descendants to care for their welfare.

iii) Protection. But much of the care for ancestor spirits is carried out for purely selfish reasons. The spirit retains his human temperament, and a hungry or neglected spirit can be very ill-tempered and vengeful. It pays to meet every whim of the spirits.

b) Social Function. In the words of J.T. Addison:

As a stimulus to morality, ancestor worship has been powerful. Conscious that they live and act in the sight of ancestors, the Chinese instinctively refer to them as judges of their conduct. To the ordinary social motives they add the desire to live worthy of their forebears and the fear of committing acts that would dishonour them .... These sanctions serve to heighten the moral sense (1925:26).

Confucius (557-479 B.C.) accepted the moral and social values of this custom but rejected the religious "superstition" associated with it. He tried to purge out the religious aspects while retaining the moral values (Yang 1961:45). Only a small intellectual elite folllowed the Confucian pattern. The common people continued to serve the spirits. The Chinese of the Nanyang (Southeast Asia) are of common stock. Their "kowtow" (reverential kneeling) before the living elders and before the ancestor tablets is called "pai" (worship). They normally make no distinction between the social and religious aspects of filial piety, and where the inroads of modern thought erode the religious beliefs, so also are traditional moral values eroded, much to·the consternation of the national leadership of Singapore. The Chinese values of respect for elders, loyalty, submission, service of others, interdependence and upholding the honour of the family, are all bound up in this intricate family system which believes that the ancestors are watching and will revenge and reward according to adherence to these traditional values.

*The Family as Context for Church Growth.* The traditional family system has great relevance for the growth of the church. Let me illustrate this in seven areas.

First, Robert Bolton found in Taiwan that where there was an extended family it was more difficult to make converts, and especially to get a decision to destroy the idols (Swanson 1978:24). Conversely, if there was a general People Movement, the wider the network, the greater would be the potential for conversion. Certainly in Singapore the old Chinese women are the persecutors of young converts and the chief active resisters of the gospel. But because of the predominance of single nucleus families, young couples can go their own way without being watched over and intimidated by mothers and mothers in law. They can make their own decisions more freely. In Singapore, there is a definite People Movement, but it is taking place more in the peer group based networks than in families, and so the single nucleus family is generally more advantageous for the gospel.

Having said that, I must hurry on to make a second point. The family network, though weakening due to the encroachment of modern values, is still very significant and an important potential base for Christianity. The use of the Chinese home and the networks of relatives has been utilized by some churches very fruitfully. Our Saviour's Anglican Church has special teams mobilized to work on evangelizing relatives of church people. They minister to the family both spiritually and physically when there is a crisis such as illness or a death. As a result of this approach, they have been seeing an encouraging number of conversions of older Chinese Religionists.

In another church, when the conversion of an elder or person of high status takes place, the pastor is quick to start a Christian meeting in his home to take advantage of his authoritative position in various networks, for the spread of the gospel.

In an extensive study done by the Southern Baptists in Malaysia and Singapore, it was found that the most common request for help by members was for training in how to evangelize family members. While the family network is still strong, young people are of such a different mindset, and so limited in their use of the old dialects, that they find it well nigh impossible to take advantage of the family network for evangelism. Such aids as dialect tapes, literature, and language development courses need to be provided by churches to help young Christians in this unique mission field.

Third, with all the modern pressures breaking up the family, the church should be the champion of the family. It should also provide within its own life the community and sense of cohesion that many Singaporeans are finding the family no longer provides. The church should be a place of belonging. In my *Twelve Churches Study* I found that herein lay probably the single largest area of failure at the present time. Of those attending church, many expressed a strong felt need for friendship and community. Among the drop-outs surveyed, there was an overwhelming sense of bitterness toward the church for advertising herself as "body" and then failing to demonstrate a body life. Here is a need arising from the national context, and we must begin to develop dynamics that will provide for this social dimension of belonging. In my paper on Chinese Festivals, some detailed suggestions are given as to how the church might foster family cohesion while at the same time forwarding the cause of the gospel and strengthening the cohesiveness of the church (Hinton 1983).

Fourth, there has been a lack of intimacy and expressed affection in the traditional Chinese home. The father of the house is especially aloof; even young children are seldom fondled. The display of affection between husbands and wives is rare. Traditionally, love was not demonstrated in expressions of affection but had to be inferred from acts of sacrificial service such as a mother's care for her children. This situation is partly a result of the Buddhist concern for detachment from desire, and partly a product of the system of hierarchy and submission within the family. Alan Gates observes it in Taiwan (1966:131, 158), Nyce in Malaysia (1970:49), and Stephen Neill notes a similar attitude in Japanese society. Two things must be observed in relation to this Chinese reserve. Firstly, the younger generation, influenced by western films and customs, desire more overt expression of affection and concern such as parents kissing their children and saying "please" when commanding them. Teenagers want to feel loved and have more proof of their parents' love. Older members of the family are not usually open to this change of custom and so the church has been turned to as an agent advertising herself as community and a centre of warm fellowship. The problem is that church members are, of course, themselves products of the same tradition; all desire affection and intimacy, but find it personally hard to express it. People often come to the church because of her self-confessed fellowship base, but become disappointed and resentful if they do not find the warmth for which they hoped. In my *Twelve Churches Study*, questionnaires returned from dropouts frequently referred to the "hypocrisy" of church people in this regard. Secondly, the church urgently needs to work at exercises to help Chinese Christians express their feelings, so that they can grow in this dimension, for the affective domain is a legitimate and important part of religion which the church has, with her intellectual emphasis, neglected.

Fifth, because of the collapse of the home as the centre for teaching and enforcing moral values, the church must become the teacher and bastion of morality while at the same time helping her people set up homes that, true to Chinese tradition, are themselves centres of moral and social control.

Further, in traditional rural China where little ever changed, the knowledge of the older people was superior, but in modern Singapore, young people are better educated and frequently better paid than their parents. In this situation the church needs to help her young members in the delicate task of fulfilling the biblical mandate to respect and obey their parents while, at the same time, maintaining their status as responsible adults who cannot be subject to every whim of an old and sometimes bigoted and unenlightened parent or grandparent.

Finally, the church must not allow herself to become inadvertently an agent of western individualism as she so often has done. At this time, when many Singaporeans are insecure and a little disoriented due to the reduced social role of the family, society can ill afford large doses of western individualism.

## The Role of Women in Religion

Mothers are the traditional transmitters of Chinese Religion, and they are the most active in the day to day observance of religious rituals such as offering food on the family altar and burning joss-sticks morning and evening. This sexual bias in religious activity comes, I believe, because Chinese women are in charge of the household affairs, while the men run the family businesses. Traditional religion is mostly related to family matters which are the woman's responsibility. If the children are sick or upset, it is she who makes the offerings, seeks a medium or goes to the temple for healing or to appease the offended spirits.

A study done by sociologist Joseph Tamney found that more women perceived themselves as religious than did men (1970a:249).

This study also showed that women were dropping out of Chinese Religion faster than men, and that they were adopting Christianity far more readily than the men; many of the latter tending to say they had no religion (1970a:268). These details throw considerable light on what is happening within Christianity.

First, the church has a major problem of imbalance between males and females. In my *Twelve Churches Study* I found an overall pattern of 42 per cent male and 58 per cent female. While churches varied considerably in their male-female ratio, those growing fastest with new converts were taking in far more females than males, so this is a current phenomenon. In a society where singleness is still unacceptable and parents still have some say in the marriage of daughters, this imbalance is a contributor to the attrition rate in the church and so will be studied in depth in chapter 11. We can observe at this point, however, that one reason for the imbalance could be that as women are traditionally more religiously active, when they lose confidence in traditional religion they more actively seek an alternative, whereas males, who allow females to cary out family religion on their behalf, more easily slip from passive belief to passive agnosticism. The church here faces a problem that is at least partly contextual.

Second, not infrequently the wife or mother is the first older member of the family to convert to Christianity. This is probably because of her active religious bent.

Third, often because she is looked to as the religious authority in the home, she can influence the older men of the home to convert even though she is technically of lesser status than they. This of course may only happen over a period of time, but we should not underestimate the significance and influence of women in our evangelistic effort.

Finally, while in Chinese Religion women are often religious leaders, mediums and diviners, in the church they are largely relegated to menial housekeeping tasks and Sunday school teaching. To this point only the charismatics appear to have began to tap more fully the capacity of women in religious leadership, and to give public scope for their often strong intuitive capacity to hear and discern the voice of the Lord.

## Leadership and Authority

While there is a close correlation between the Chinese attitudes to authority and leadership and to traditional kinship structures, we will deal with this important subject separately.

Harold Fickett declares that there are three requirements for a healthy church: leadership, leadership and leadership. Yet leadership in the churches of Singapore is a puzzle, to me at least, and is the locus of many problems. Donald McGavran frequently mentions the high level of training and high salaries of pastors as an obstacle to growth (1980:163). The converse is equally true.

Among the Chinese one would expect great honour to be given to religious workers, but that does not appear to be the case. All too frequently pastors are poorly paid, little respected and largely without authority to lead. For example, in one typical church where 265 questionnaires were returned, I found that the only male in the congregation whose salary was less than S$500 per month was the church worker. Another young pastor complained that he could not afford to get married on a salary of S$350 per month, and this two years after the government census showed that the average income of a male employee was S$677 per month and the self-employed male, S$803 (Khoo 1981a). A study of Chinese churches in Taiwan revealed a similar situation. It was discovered that the average pastor's salary was 50 per cent less than the national average wage, and 13 per cent of church members felt that their pastor should not be allowed a day of rest each week. Many more doubted his right to an annual vacation. In fact, few churches offered their pastors annual leave and most pastors would never dare to ask for a holiday (Swanson 1981:131-132, 149). A Baptist study in Singapore and Malaysia did not reveal quite the same degree of need among Baptists though many pastors did feel financially insecure (Baptist Mission 1975:21-22). When in a prosperous society many pastors are virtual beggars, depending in times of illness and crisis on the personal charity of church members, there is a real problem to be overcome.

After puzzling over this anomaly for some years I am coming to believe that the root of this problem, which is driving many pastors to despair and eventual escape into secular employment, is found in the area of traditional Chinese values.

*The Monk in Chinese Society.* Monks have never been greatly respected. The masses had little place for the monasteries and institutional religion. The vast majority of men and women who entered the monasteries did so because they had failed to cope with life — the illiterate poor, jilted lovers, bankrupt business-men. In a heavily materialistic society, such escape brought them little honour. Monasteries were so poorly endowed that monks were forced into the streets to beg. In more recent times such poverty has been romanticized and one often hears in the church that poverty among religious workers is a sign of spirituality. Enforced spirituality? Tamney quotes an article from a Taiwan newspaper, dated 1967, which begins by lumping monks and priests together with prostitutes, actors, roaming traders and porters (1970a:258). They have come to be seen as ignorant, unthinking performers of passed down religious rituals. Some of this reputation has rubbed off on to pastors who have often had limited education. By comparison, it is interesting to note that in Korea the pastor is seen in terms of the Confucian teacher model with the result that he is highly esteemed and usually well paid.

*The Ruling Elite.* The institutions of Chinese society have always been hierarchical or pyramid-shaped. There was, and still is in Singapore, a ruling elite and a power elite who influence the rulers. Clearly the religious worker belongs at the bottom, not at the top of the pyramid. No matter how well trained the pastor might be, the crucial decisions within most churches are made by a small ruling elite over whom the pastor has limited influence. These are usually the successful and monied business-men and executives. In the denominations with an imported synodal system of government, the pastor has been able to wrest a little more power from the ruling elite, but even there we find limited modification of the Chinese system. In 1982, the newly appointed Anglican bishop of Singapore came into office, not from the ranks of the clergy but directly from his position as medical superintendent of one of the largest national hospitals.

*Rule by Elders.* In rural China the elders of society and the family held great sway, and that pattern is still greatly evident in the churches of Singapore. In traditional society which was marked by slow change, the elders were by experience well equipped to lead. But in modern, fast changing urban society, where young people are usually better educated and more in tune with the times than their leaders, there is frequent tension. The church has been slow to give younger members positions of authority unless they have lacked older members to lead. Older leaders have tended to be conservative, resistant to innovation and unadventurous in the cause of the gospel.

The young moderns are impatient, optimistic and eager, and frequent stonewalling by elders has forced the Chinese independent spirit into active expressions of rebellion time and again. Schism is common. Not that schisms are always totally bad. While they do leave wounds and ill feeling, they often result also in the same rapid growth as does planned church planting. For a typical example, one CNEC church has now had three breakaway groups and the mother and all three offspring are thriving. In fact, the mother church, with a healthy DGR of 473 per cent has, in five years, been outgrown by one of her daughters.

*Style of Leadership.* The traditional pattern of Chinese authority has been characterized by autocratic direction, hierarchy, respect for and rule by elders. Leadership has been based on ascription rather than achievement, and marked by the repetition of past ways. The new generation has been influenced by a new set of values with more emphasis on democratic patterns, free, creative thinking, and often such a degree of orientation to the future and change that the "new" tends to be expected to be better than the old. The old and the new clash, with the old *ruling* rather than *leading, forcing* its goals on members in military manner rather than *selling* them. Responsibility is not easily delegated, and so little room is left for initiative in the tasks allotted to the rank and file.

In spite of the resentment of the young towards this style of leadership and despite all the western influences to which they are exposed, it is always surprising how younger Chinese quickly revert to the traditional Chinese pattern when they themselves become leaders, tending to become equally as autocratic as their forebears.

Their Chinese reserve makes it difficult for them to express warmth, praise and appreciation. Thus the rank and file who serve in the church commonly lack positive encouragement. Only negative feedback filters down from above; criticism when things go wrong. This is very dispiriting.

***Implications of Traditional Leadership for Church Growth.*** While the traditional, autocratic expression of leadership is increasingly unacceptable with the new generation, young people do need to realize that strong leadership is essential for maximum growth. Congregational government tends not to grow progressive churches. On the other hand, elders must recognize that, while leadership needs to be firm or strong, it must also be unified, flexible, visionary and with its ear to the ground. All too often churches have elders of equal strength and they bog down in change-resistant bureaucracy which is even more stultifying than government by the congregation.

Second, leadership style needs to move along the continuum from ruling toward leading.

Third, in a changing world there must be a growing recognition of achievement and training. Pastors should be allowed to rise to a place of leadership if they have the gifts and capacity to do so.

Fourth, the old monk-beggar mentality has to go. No pastor can function at his best when dogged by poverty, a poor self-image and a low level of respect. He should be paid a reasonable salary, the stewardship of which should thereafter be a private matter between him and the Lord. Keeping him poor will reduce his effectiveness, result in damaging attitudes, cause his wife and children to become resentful and will certainly not make him more spiritual!

Fifth, the pastor's motives for entering the ministry must be respected. It is almost never a monkish escape from worldly failure. But, at the same time, when pastors are given so little scope to develop, the most talented Chinese are going to continue to be reluctant to enter the ministry.

Next, the church needs to come to terms with the biblical qualifications for church leadership. These are not secular success, a Ph.D., family contacts or hoary age per se.

Finally, because of the keen desire of many zealous young Christians to serve the Lord, they serve in the church, but do not serve the church. There is a tendency to feel they are serving the Lord in the church in spite of the leadership, not in partnership with it. They pay only lip service to the curricula and rules set by the church. They are doing their own thing because of a lack of praise or perks from the leadership. The less hardy get discouraged and become passive or drop out.

Old customs and patterns of thought die hard and we cannot expect change overnight. But change must come if the harvest is not to be lost. There needs to be sensitive teaching on Christian leadership, and Ted Engstrom's *The Making of a Christian Leader* would provide an excellent starting point for facilitating such change.

## Conservatism

One cannot discuss traditional Chinese ways without mentioning conservatism. Nature religion is a religion of the status quo, of nonprogression, with no climax and no end. Interest is in preserving order, not in progress. Harmony with the unchangeable forces is deemed the path of the wise; it is the core value of the Chinese worldview.

Not only has this value tended to hold the church back from venturesome and visionary developments for the sake of the Kingdom, but it has preserved orthodox evangelical theology which, as mentioned earlier, is a positive church growth factor. Liberal theology places the root of causality in the natural rather than the supernatural, something the Chinese find hard to accept. Liberal theology also has had little appeal because it tends to speak of social issues and social action, where traditional Chinese religious interest is much more individualistic and egocentric. The evangelical message, for better and worse, is quietist and personal rather than social. Furthermore, Liberalism is a theology of doubt and, I believe for that reason, has lacked appeal to a generation exiting their traditional religion because it lacked credibility and certainty. The more dogmatic evangelical faith is more attractive. In fact, church growth statistics would indicate that the more dogmatic and restrictive a system, the greater its appeal.

In summary then we may say that the traditions of the Chinese Religionist have had and still do have a profound effect on church growth. Those five thousand year old values and patterns are still a significant part of the milieu in which the Kingdom of God is being built. But it is one that is being radically challenged by modernity and government policy and programme. It is to the new and developing social context that we now turn our attention.

## For discussion

1.a    Consider the non-Christian members of your family or among your close acquaintances and try to analyze the reasons that are keeping them from becoming Christians.
1.b    Can you suggest specific ways whereby these barriers might be broken down?
1.c    Is there anything in the old value-system which can be utilized as a contact point in presenting the Gospel (e.g. fear of spirits, the search for prosperity)?
2.a    Discuss the characteristics of Chinese Religion outlined on pages 33-34 and list the ways these basic attitudes and values affect the church for good or ill.
2.b    How can the church, through its ministry and practice, utilize the positive values and counter the negative attitudes which are the heritage of the old religion?

# Chapter 4
# Singapore: The Modern City

> Church Growth does not take place in a vacuum. It occurs in an enormously complex society ... Society is constantly changing. Society is a revolution. Each generation establishes a new place for itself ... Society is not an unchanging mosaic. It is a kaleidoscope. Every piece is on an express train. Many pieces are going in different directions. This is the social reality (McGavran 1981: 290).

So said Donald McGavran of American cities and church growth. And if that degree of change and complexity is true of American cities, it is even more so of modernizing, pluralistic Singapore.

## Growing Churches Recognize Social Realities

We have observed the powerful influence of traditional culture and religion on Singaporeans and church growth. This is the "cultural hinterland" which acts in resistance to the new values and life styles that are emerging in the modernizing city. And it is the new, in all its urban complexity, which is to be the subject of the following three chapters, as we seek to understand the influence of this rapidly changing milieu upon the church.

Dayton and Fraser comment further on the importance of

understanding the social realities and complex social networks of industrial urban society, explaining that

> Receptivity to the gospel is a function of the "fit" that exists between the gospel and the culture as well as the satisfaction people presently feel with the current fate in life that culture provides for them.
> [In fact] the political, social and economic context sometimes can be so overbearing that they become the primary definers of the life of a people (1980:110).

I personally am convinced that the sociological and anthropological phenomena we shall observe are of such positive significance at the present moment in Singapore that a church must be very bad indeed from an institutional point of view if it is not to grow. The modern context has created what I believe to be a remarkably receptive soil for the seed of the gospel. The church is already reaping a great harvest, but it is evident that possibly half of the potential harvest is still being lost to secularism because we do not have enough labourers active in the harvest field, and the present task force is not adequately sensitive to the nature of the social realities in which they are working. We cannot generalize about the way to redeem a city. Each urban church must tailor its pattern of harvesting to its own particular context.

Cities have been much maligned both by Christian and sociological writers, and in this chapter I wish to clear away some of the smog of misunderstanding. Unless urban church workers have both a true view of and a positive attitude towards the city, their ministry will be less than effective. Having cleared the air a little on this matter, I then wish to sketch the programme of revolutionary change that is being so boldly implemented in Singapore. Then, in chapters 5 and 6, a number of specific sociological phenomena will be examined and their impact on church growth evaluated.

## The City: Good or Evil?
Speaking in very practical terms, one's view of the city is significantly shaped by a set of seldom examined presuppositions. These presuppositions influence the way we see the city and may seriously limit what we can do in and for the city.

The majority of western anthropologists and sociologists have idealized the rural style of life, taking on a firm antiurban bias. Theologians have showed a similar gloomy outlook in regard to the city. If I am not mistaken, many church workers in Singapore have inadvertently imbibed an ambivalence toward the city which is of necessity their habitat. Certainly scholarly sociological articles written by Singaporeans have frequently had a negative flavour which stems from the underlying query, "Can any good thing come out of a city?" It is important therefore that we uncover and examine those presuppositions about the city.

*Urban Anthropology and Sociology: Their Context.* The early urban anthropologists were frequently rural practitioners who followed the migrant section of the population they were studying into the city. Naturally a migrant people will face some problems while finding their feet in a new setting and culture which is greatly at variance with that of the rural homogeneous society from which they came. Any anthropologist truly involved with his people is going to be very sensitive to the disruption of their lives and the cultural dislocation they suffer.

Sociologists have commonly been funded by city planners and governments to try to discover solutions to expressions of social pathology such as divorce, crime, rape and suicide that are worrying those responsible for the city. Their focus of attention has thus been on the problems of the city.

Many of the early writers of the influential Chicago School of sociology saw the city as unnatural and artificial. Urban centres were viewed as the source of all kinds of social and personality disorganization and deviant behaviour (Eames and Goode 1977: 54). Terms such as impersonal, faceless, superficial, fragmented, anomic, dehumanizing and secularizing dominated their writings as they became taken up with the social pathology of the city. Almost every problem of modern life has been blamed on the city.

Robert Redfield placed rural and urban on a continuum, characterizing rural communities as simple, moral, integrated, personal, homogeneous, human in values and religious. The city, on the other hand, was defined as sophisticated, corrupt, immoral, disintegrated, impersonal, heterogeneous, dehumanized and irreligious. He was convinced that degeneration occurred in the move from village to city (1941:353).

Louis Wirth, in his essay "Urbanism as a Way of Life" (1938), defined the city culturally and sociologically. To him the city was "a way of life", economically successful but socially destructive, characterized by the breaking up of the family, the disappearance of neighbourhood, the undermining of traditional values, depersonalization, anomie and insecurity (Palen 1981:133).

To Robert Park the city was to be seen in terms of competition and density of living, but with cultural and moral dimensions. He observed that social control was lost with the change from primary to secondary relationships, and this, he said, was the cause of crime. Durkheim also saw the city as a centre of anomie, where traditional social controls have collapsed. For him too this loss of values and meanings was the cause of urban crime, divorce and suicide. Oswald Spengler believed that the cities were a deadly cancer in society and would eventually be self-destructing because of their own sinfulness (1928:136). More recently, Edward Banfield in The Unheavenly City (1970), blamed the city for most of the world's ills.

Such blanket condemnations of the city, while not totally absent today, are certainly less frequent. More moderate statements are the order of the day. Value can be seen in the cities, though few modern students of urban centres take a very positive stance.

**Theologians and the City.** In 1902, Abraham Cowley made a statement which could well sum up the general feeling of theologians over the years. He said, "God the first garden made, and the first city Cain" (Palen 1981:73). Jacques Ellul, French professor of law, city mayor and lay theologian, takes issue with all those who hold high hopes for the city and man's capacity to turn it into an instrument for good. In his book The Meaning of the City, he shows the city as the creation of man; the city is "the world" in which the church is imprisoned. It is an advance against God and stands under His condemnnation (1970:13, 16, 47). He traces the history of the city in the Bible from Cain to Nimrod to Sodom, Nineveh, Babylon and Jerusalem which crucified the Saviour. The picture he paints is one of gloom, confusion, inhumanity, non-communication and strife. His emphasis is more prophetic than redemptive, but he does, however, note that on occasion God has a positive redemptive role for the city. Despite its vices, God does still adopt a city for His purpose. According to Ellul, we must, like the prophets, proclaim first the judgment of God upon the city and then the truth that God is going to create a different and lasting city for man (1970:77, 181). While this book breaks new ground in developing a theology of the city, one cannot but feel that Ellul's own experience in law and with city management has influenced him to place undue emphasis on the disorderliness and seaminess of city life.

Most Christian writers, while not stating their view of the city explicitly, nevertheless reflect a rather pessimistic attitude toward it, and this mood has passed over into the general Christian community.

David Watson, describing the urban evangelistic context of the church, quotes almost entirely from authors who are critical of the city. Words and phrases of a negative nature predominate: "both apathy and violence"; "the intractable problems of pollution"; "over-population, the experts issue warning after warning, and forecast disaster after disaster"; "the unspoken fear is the increasing depersonalization of the individual"; "that sense of deprivation is made greater and more compelling by the anonymity and humiliation of the crowded, complex, rundown city areas"; "the probability is that violence will increase as cities grow"; and "the incidence of violence is almost perfectly correlated with the size of the city!" (1977:16). Such a catalogue of gloom cannot but deposit a residue of antibodies toward the city in the mind of the reader.

Harvey Cox would be the most widely known exception to this characteristic Christian outlook on the city. In *The Secular City*, he presents the city as the demonstration of men's coming of age, of his being able to manage his own affairs. To him, the city is not a place of rootlessness and alienation, but is the situation where the old cyclical agricultural patterns are disrupted, so liberating man to move forward with God to *progress*. He does not see the city as anonymous but as the place of *liberation* from old relationships and social controls so that people may be themselves. As evangelicals, we would beg to differ with Cox's equation of the city with the Kingdom of God (1965:109,

116), but we need to realize that the phenomena of the city can be seen through other eyes than those of unrelieved gloom.

How then should we view the city and the church within the city?

***Toward a Biblical View of the Church in the City.*** Frequently the Bible portrays cities as evil — Babel, Sodom and Gomorrah, Nineveh, the cities of Canaan and Babylon. But cities are also depicted as symbols of God's presence and care — the cities of refuge and Jerusalem. Cities are, in fact, used in Scripture to epitomize both evil (Babylon — Rev. 17:5) and good (the New Jerusalem coming out of heaven — Rev. 21:2, 10-27).

It would appear to me that there are three matters that affect the quality of city life negatively. The first is that of human nature. A city is a concentration of people and thus will have dimensions of concentrated sinfulness. There will be excesses of evil, but there should be also corresponding possibilities of the combining of human resources of goodness. The second factor is that of organization and management. To this point in time man has generally managed his cities very poorly. With the irreversible urbanization of the world, will man's increased experience in structuring and management of the modern city result in better and happier cities? In theory at least this should be so though the dimensions of population increase and urban pluralism create a mammoth challenge. Third, new residents in a city are of necessity going to pass through a period of adjustment, insecurity and possible negative reactions. The recognition of these three sources of disruption falls far short of condemning a city as evil per se. These problems and urban evils do not imply that the city is inherently worse than the country which has been characterized by unbelievable poverty, restriction and a static lifestyle. The city has its own values and rewards; broad companionship, stimulation, freedom, prosperity and more (Rooy 1979:177).

Whatever the empirical state of cities in the Bible or today, there is no doubt whatsoever that God wills the redemption of the city. He holds out hope for the city. Jesus was incarnated into a city. He went about preaching in all the cities (Mt 9:35). The Spirit of God directed the early missionaries of the church to cities — Antioch, Lystra, Derby, Iconium, Corinth and Rome. And the history of God's redemptive purpose is pictured as climaxing and culminating in the city of God — the New Jerusalem.

The church is called to be salt, light and leaven in the city. Our mission is not to pluck people from the city as Lot was saved from Sodom. Nor are we, with Cox, to dream of turning the city into the Kingdom. The mission of the church is an intermediate one. The church is to be in the city a microcosm of Kingdom *koinonia*. But more than that, the reconciling power of Christ should begin to touch the city itself and to transform it. In the city with its vast hoards of people, the intensification of human relationships, the ethnic plurality and linguistic babel, there is a greater potential for chaos, hatred and sin than there ever was in rural areas, but there is also a greater potential for order, love, unity and godly community than the world has ever known. The opportunities for manifestations of the unifying love of Christ, and reconciliation through the empowering of the Spirit are unprecedented. And having carried out its witness in the city and, in part, transformed the city into the likeness of the heavenly city, the church has prepared men and nature for residence in that eternal city whose builder and maker is God (Rooy 1979:180-181).

The city is worth saving. The city must be saved. Having come to that conclusion, the churches of the city are then prepared to begin to map out strategies for its salvation. The diversity and complexity of the city means that no single approach will be right in all places. Hope for uniting mankind in the family of Christ, in one vast *koinonia*, lies in a mosaic of complementary approaches. The ultimate unity will come through diversity.

We must now begin to look at the nature of modern Singapore as city.

## Singapore's Leap into the Future

Asia has one of the longest standing traditions of city dwelling. In fact, 200 years ago Asia had more city dwellers than the rest of the world put together. These ancient cities were of the pre-industrial type, primarily political, cultural and defence centres, frequently inland and walled. But outside of Japan, China and ndia, almost all the Asian cities are of more recent colonial origin. Such cities include Hong Kong, Singapore, Manila and Jakarta as well as Calcutta and Bombay in India, and Shanghai in China. Commonly these colonial cities were "primate cities", principal cities which overwhelmed all other urban centres in the country. Normally, because their chief purpose was trade in relation to the motherland across the seas, they were port cities. Although on Asian soil, their roots and patterns were largely western. Many of these cities were a merging of European colonialism with Chinese urbanness (Palen 1981:347-351, 401-402, 421).

But the similarity of Singapore to the other Asian cities largely ends here. Urban anthropologist John Palen cites Singapore as atypical, the urban exception to the various aspects of urban gloom he then goes on to describe.

Most western cities developed in responses to industrialization and so had a solid economic base. By contrast, most Third World cities grew without economic self-sufficency. The withdrawal of the colonialists, especially when occurring suddenly as a result of revolution, threw these cities into acute economic crisis. To complicate matters, most experienced, and continue to experience, a flood of uninvited migrants from their rural hinterlands. These cities have, despite many attempts, been unable to seal themselves off and so control their growth. Further, the modernization of a populace without an industrial base leads to serious inflation and economic trouble. When people acquire a taste for the modern way of life before their nation has developed its own industry, catastrophe is imminent. In the case of Singapore, the withdrawal of the British was gradual and planned. The large Chinese majority, energetically and profitably involved in trade and commerce, provided substantial economic stability. Then again, as an island nation, it had no rural hinterland and was therefore not hopelessly swamped by hoards of impoverished migrants. It also succeeded in controlling its own internal population growth. Finally, it was able to establish industry to supplement its entrepot trade and to support the growing taste for modern living.

## The Singapore Master Plan

In 1960, as Singapore began to find its feet as an independent nation, it faced five problems of gigantic proportions: the vast urban slum, the chronic high level of unemployment, endemic crime and gangsterism, population explosion and the lack of a national identity. To these five a sixth was added later: the need for a moral basis. The new government set about developing plans and programmes designed for success in these areas.

In 1959, the People's Action Party (PAP) formed the first national government and began to draw up a Master Plan which co-ordinated and regulated all phases of city development. The planners viewed the city aesthetically, wanting a clean, green and beautiful city. They also planned the city for technical efficiency. City design included the careful correlating of industrial zones with housing within the financial reach of unskilled and semi-skilled workers. Traffic flow and transport were integrated into the plan. John Palen laments the failure of most American urban master plans as too idealistic, static and stylized, and unable to be implemented in a laissez-faire society (1981: 318, 322). But the PAP saw the need for control if wholistic visions for the city were to become a reality. Singapore adopted a modified form of socialism. The government is democratic, but has gained so much of the popular vote that in practice a one party system has developed. The achievements of Singapore's government and Singaporeans have been astounding. I propose to survey briefly their plans and achievements.

**Urban Renewal.** During the period 1819-1926, the population grew rapidly and the inner city turned into an enormous slum known as Chinatown. In 1927, the colonial government formed the Singapore Improvement Trust (SIT) to deal with this problem, but its powers were so limited that in 32 years it built only 20,907 units. When the PAP came to power in 1959, one of its first projects was to plan and implement a national housing and urban renewal programme. In 1960 it formed the Housing Development Board (HDB) and Urban Renewal Authority (URA), the former being for building housing and the latter for slum clearance, city planning and re-zoning.

*Public housing.* The density of the slum was such that an average of seven new housing units was needed to clear one shophouse. The government set to work. It estimated that in the next ten years private enterprise could build 40,000 units, and so set a target for the HDB to build, in the same time, 110,000 units in high-rise apartment blocks. By the end of 1970, the target had been exceeded by 10,000 units (Teh 1975:1-21). This programme has gone on until, in 1984, 75 per cent of the population is living in public housing.

The long waiting list of people opting for government rather than private housing reflects the outstanding success of this project. In 1981/82 alone the number of applicants on the waiting list increased by 35 per cent. To have the Chinese in particular decide to forfeit their traditional need to have their own plot of land is no small vote of confidence in government housing and socialization programmes. Surveys of residents also reflect a remarkable level of satisfaction with the new housing.

**Urban Planning.** With such limited space, land use has had to be watched carefully. Public high density housing and government controls have effectively stopped what would have become suburban sprawl swallowing up the city's green. In 1967 there began a programme of levelling hills and buying soil from Indonesia to build out from the shores and thus enlarge Singapore's land area. The target of a 10 per cent increase in land mass through reclamation is now almost achieved. Estuaries are being dammed off, drained of sea-water and turned into reservoirs in order to reduce the city's dependence on imported water from Malaysia. Only about 55 per cent of the island can eventually be built upon because of the land needed for water catchment, military purposes, recreation and so forth. In response to continuous studies of public housing, greater attention is being given to design, atmosphere and amenities. Blocks that were thrown up to meet the urgent needs of the early 1960s are being remodelled, and high density areas thinned by demolition of some blocks.

Old Singapore grew largely undirected in a concentric circle manner. But the new Singapore is being developed on what Palen calls "a nuclei sector approach". Jurong is being developed as the largest industrial estate with a companion housing estate nearby consisting of appropriate level housing. Most of the housing is developed in new towns, some of which are inhabited by as many as 250,000 people. These are further divided into communities of 6,000-7,000 people. Each community or neighbourhood is provided with its own amenities: shops, hawkers' centre, clinics and so on, while larger areas share sports complexes, theatres, schools, libraries, child-care and counselling services.

Land use in residential areas is only 13 per cent and special effort has been made to provide a green environment, even to the point of planting large, pre-grown shady trees by the use of heavy duty cranes. The clean, green, fresh appearance of Singapore, "the Garden City", never fails to draw admiring comments from western tourists and it has made Singaporeans proud of their nation. Even air-pollution has been so controlled that despite industrialization, pollution levels have dropped each year since 1970. Man has always dreamed of creating the perfect city. While Singapore is not Utopia, its amazing success has, not surprisingly, made it a focus of study for town planners worldwide.

*Economic Development.* Singapore had prospered by entrepot trade, but the PAP realized that this could not be relied upon as a stable economic base because it left Singapore too vulnerable to the political and economic ebb and flow of neighbouring countries. Nor could it sustain modernization. Thus, while continuing to encourage shipping and trade, the government inaugurated an all-out drive to industrialize. Its own housing programme served to create demand for materials and to alleviate the previously chronic unemployment problem.

Despite many economic incentives, such as ten-year tax exemptions, the Chinese with their tradition of small independent businesses proved unwilling to invest their capital in larger consortiums which were not totally under their own individual control. Not to be beaten, the government, using money from the Central Provident Fund (a compulsory retirement fund which now extracts 25 per cent of the worker's salary, supplemented by another 25 per cent from the employer), began investing in industry. It carried out some projects alone, and also entered into joint ventures with multinational and foreign companies. The Raffles City Project with its 70-storey hotel, shops and conference centres, the Singapore Airlines, the Development Bank of Singapore and the Petrochemicals industry are just a few of the key developments made possible through government capital. Today manufacturing is the backbone of the economy and Chinese businessmen are learning that industry can be a safe and profitable place to invest their capital. Financial and business services are second only to manufacturing as a source of revenue; Singapore has become a financial centre for Asia. The largest single export item now is petrochemicals which, for a country with no oil of its own, is quite surprising. In 1980, external trade increased by 34 per cent. Against a backdrop of world recession, Singapore's economy has grown uninterruptedly showing annual double digit real increases in the Gross Domestic Product.

The situation has so improved that the government is able to select the type of industry it feels suits Singapore's low natural resource, full-employment, land-scarce situation. It is encouraging small land use, high-tech industries which are highly automated and non-polluting. Industries deemed undesirable or of low efficiency are being forced out. Land intensive industries are being encouraged to move to neighbouring countries, from where value still accrues to Singapore. The drive for efficiency and high-tech industry is showing results. In 1980 the productivity rate of labour doubled, the production of electronics increased 36 per cent and that of precision instruments 21 per cent. The emphasis on manufacturing has not hurt the entrepot trade. In fact, Singapore has recently become the second busiest port in the world.

In her drive for self-sufficiency, intensive, low land-use farming methods are being developed. By these methods Singapore now produces 100 per cent of her eggs and pork and 78 per cent of her poultry needs. Vegetables are being cultivated intensively using hydroponics. Aquaculture and fisheries in coastal waters are now supplying a quarter of the nation's seafood needs. These material achievements are truly remarkable.

**Making the city safe.** In this respect also, the government finally succeeded. Undoubtedly the cleaning up of the slums, the rise in standard of living and the wider opportunities for education and employment all contributed to success. However, strong measures were needed before the stranglehold of the secret societies and gangs on society was broken.

**Population Control.** Most Asian nations have been unable to bring their population growth under control. But once again,

Singapore's efforts have met with success. In the mid-1950s the annual birthrate was 4.3 per cent. Twenty years later it had fallen to 1.3 per cent and is on target to reach zero growth by the year 2030. Responsible for this change is the Singapore Family Planning and Population Board. Through publicity, incentives and disincentives, the rate of contraception has risen to 71 per cent, the highest in South East Asia.

It should be noted, however, that from a Christian point of view, some of the methods used to achieve this end may be seriously questioned and their long-term effects on society harmful. For instance, the church can never condone abortion as a means of birth control.

*The Search for a National Identity.* For national cohesion, national security and overall impetus for development, a nation must have a national identity. But Singapore faced a dilemma in this area. Decolonized peoples have three major options in their search for identity. They can regress to their precolonial cultural roots. But Singapore had no precolonial history and has always been culturally pluralistic. A regressive identity for Singapore could only be to create a third China, which would inevitably lead to internal racial turmoil and be unacceptable to her non-Chinese neighbours. The second alternative is to follow the colonial, capitalistic way, but most nations are too proud to follow the ways of their oppressors. The third option is to react against capitalism and its oppression of the masses and opt for a socialist identity. For Singapore the slightest turn to a pinker left would destroy her chance of industrialization and would halt her trade; the flow of western capital and technology would dry up and her trading neighbours would cut her off.

Singapore's solution was to attempt to create a "non-ideological identity", which in short meant an identity through an "ideology of pragmatism" aimed always at national prosperity. The HDB flats, Jurong industrial estate, and "keep Singapore clean" campaigns became symbols of this identity (Chan and Evers 1978:117-119).

By the mid-1970s, questions and criticisms began to mount. It appeared to many that Singapore's identity had been lost by default. Industrialization had, with lightning speed, elevated Singapore to the status of a "developed nation". But the exposure to the West that had been involved in modernizing raised the question as to whether there was in her anything intrinsically Singaporean, or was she purely a western imitation (Ho Wing Meng 1976a:110-115). Some cried out that her pragmatism had sold her out to the god "moneytheism". Others, on witnessing the demolition of quaint Chinatown and like areas of traditional culture and colour, lamented that, "Singapore hasn't got any culture." (Wee Teong Boo 1976:145-146).

A new identity needed to be found that would not only be acceptable to all four ethnic and linguistic communities, but would serve to unify them into a nation, and so overcome the racial tensions of the past. Debate on this issue is by no means over, and the government appears not to have been able to settle on a safe and viable national culture and identity. But its actions and statements indicate the general direction in which it is trying to move. Assimilation is out of the question, even if ethically acceptable. "Multiracialism" and "multicultural society" are terms frequently heard. At all festivals authorities are careful to stage a cultural presentation that includes items from each of the major ethnic groups. Government leaders often speak of national unity and cultural diversity, of embracing western technology and eastern cultural values together in a truly Singaporean identity. Harmonious co-existence and the preservation of some ethnic customs appears to be the hope. There seems to be an expectation of a "stewpot type" solution where a mixture of various cultural elements takes place to form "a uniquely Singaporean culture". There are others who even appear to dream of a total melting down of all parts into some yet undefined national culture. At a cultural show, the Minister of Social Affairs said,

> We can all help in blending of a cultural alloy which will have permanent and enduring appeal to all Singaporeans. The different races must learn to be tolerant and appreciative of one another's philosophies and traditions before we can integrate culturally (Benjamin 1976:121).

Meanwhile, in a dual search for survival and identity, the government proceeds to implement policies which indicate the hoped-for direction.

First, despite criticisms of moneytheism, and accusations that

Singapore is becoming a harsh, heartless society that knows no finer values, the government continues to feel obliged to make productivity, competitiveness and meritocracy the chief values. For, as it rightly points out, although Singapore has now attained prosperity a spirit of complacency and self-indulgence will bring about her downfall because, lacking natural material resources, she will always have to depend on the quick wit and effort of her only resource, her people.

Second, the government has implemented a policy of bilingualism for Singapore. The expressed aim is that each person should speak English, the language of technology and means to economic progress as well as an acceptable common medium of communication between the ethnic groups. Then for the non-Chinese the second language is to be the mother tongue; for the Chinese it is to be Mandarin. This is designed to help preserve traditional moral values and customs, the hoped-for backbone of Singaporean culture. The widespread use of English is certainly helping to break down ethnic isolation, reduce misunderstanding and the false conceptions held by one group of another. Whether traditional values and culture can be salvaged in face of the bombardment of ideas and values that come to Singapore from all around the world is doubtful. While traditional cultural dances and music are presented at national festivals and exhibited to tourists, people are increasingly developing tastes for entertainment and music that are quite different.

The government has also implemented a policy of desegregated housing. Public flats are assigned by lot and are deliberately racially mixed. Schooling also has been desegregated. This constant exposure to other ethnic groups from childhood is having a profound effect. Ethnically mixed social groups of young people are frequently seen nowadays. It is not uncommon for young Indians to attend predominantly Chinese churches in order to be with their friends. In fact, many feel more at home in a new generation Chinese church than in an Indian church which is still bound by traditional values.

The government policy of socialization is showing remarkable results. Many people now feel more separated by class than by ethnic differences. Surveys as far back as 1970 reveal that 70 per cent of students preferred to be known as Singaporean rather than as Chinese, Indian or Malay, while 60 per cent chose Singapore as the country in which they would most like to live (Gopinathan 1976:80-81).

In spite of government exhortations to hold to the old values and cultures, there is a clear preference for the western dress, music, films and literature which is made accessible by the use of English-medium education. But whatever the shape of the "national culture" that finally emerges out of all this, the real problem of the future is going to be to keep a prosperous nation from complacency and moral degeneration.

*A Moral Base Through Education.* From the founding of the PAP, the education system has been seen as the most hopeful channel for inculcating values and building the nation. In a speech to 10,000 school teachers and principals in 1959, the newly elected Prime Minister challenged the schools with the sacred trust of building an integrated society and imparting to their students the new values deemed necessary to the survival of the new nation. In 1966 he again challenged the principals to impart suitable values such as loyalty, patriotism, tradition, the reflexes of group thinking, cohesion, stamina, endurance, discipline and love for the country. Since then the national curriculum has been repeatedly revised to incorporate these values and to enhance the socialization process. Key values in the texts are hard work, perseverance, meritocracy, competition, discipline and ruggedness. National identity has been built by the daily recitation of the oath of allegiance and participation in raising the flag as well as by civics classes. Ruggedness and discipline have further been deliberately inculcated through the National Cadet Corps in the schools, and compulsory National Service training.

The impact of this process of socialization has been profound. But, in the late 1970s, the system was given yet another challenge. There had been a noticeable increase in moral laxity, some of the new affluent generation tending toward a Bohemian lifestyle, others demonstrating a selfishness and greed that put individual preference and satisfaction before nation and even family. The elderly were being neglected. Workers were job-hopping, greedy for an extra dollar or two, uncaring about the damage widespread job-hopping did to the economy. According to government diagnosis, people were becoming callous, mercenary and totally materialistic.

The first reaction was to blame these corrupt values on the West and to charge the schools to teach moral values to the students through their various mother tongues, the mother tongue being regarded as the direct route to those Asian values which are more noble. Later, this instruction was permitted in English. However, it was not long before many people were pointing out that moral education divorced from the religious base out of which the traditional values had developed was a paper tiger. The government, in its own characteristically pragmatic way, quickly decided that religion must therefore be taught to give teeth to moral education. But which religions were to be taught? Where could instructors be found for the traditional religions, and how could proselytizing be prevented? This sensitive project is currently in the process of debate and development and is constantly undergoing refinements and amendments.

But a number of searching questions remain to be dealt with. It would appear to me that the western technology which Singapore so enthusiastically embraces, carries its own set of values — individualism, pragmatism, competition, meritocracy, elimination of the inefficient, impersonal calculation and so on. These values cannot simply be peeled away from the technology, management and financial systems and be arbitrarily replaced with traditional moral values which themselves happen to be encased in a system, one involving superstition and customs which modern Singaporeans cannot accept. The task is not so simple. Koh Tai Ann points out that Singapore has made a bogeyman out of western moral values and has idealized eastern values which are part and parcel of feudalism, social backwardness, superstition and oppression. The West also has some noble moral values such as the humanitarian spirit. The long-haired western counter-culture which Singapore despises and calls Western values is, in fact, another expression of rebellion against the same depersonalizing force of the technological culture which is impacting Singapore (1980: 292-299). Added to that, the government is strongly promoting in the schools the impartation of those so-called western values which are building economic prosperity but which are also in-
:vitably incubating the very ruthlessness and harshness that is

now deplored. It would appear that there is a conflict between the technological directives and the moral directives given to the schools. And, of course, bound up in all this is the issue of national identity. Is the nation now beginning to reap the harvest of a "non-ideological pragmatism?" Is prosperity for its own sake an adequate goal? Has materialism become a false god that has failed to truly save the nation? Such are the questions people are beginning to ask.

These questions and issues are the context of church growth in Singapore and it is not hard to see how they serve to create a most fertile soil for the evangel and open for the church a very positive arena for ministry in tune with national aspirations.

## The Church in the New Society

Let me conclude this section by naming five facets of that receptivity.

First, the government aspires to national unity without sacrificing cultural diversity. Any student of church growth would immediately affirm this as a principle of church growth, and the biblical model of the church. In fact, it has already been favourably noted in a secular study that the church is the most ethnically integrated institution in the city. In such a highly patriotic nation, every indication of the church being in tune with national goals constitutes, for the majority of people, a force for increased receptivity.

Second, the Protestant church is generally in accord with national goals. In fact, in the church there is a marked belief that prosperity is a sign of God's blessing. While such a theology is decidedly questionable, especially when it leads to a loss of a sense of responsibility to care for one's poorer neighbours, the overall harmony with government objectives is, nevertheless, a growth factor.

Third, Singapore is in search of a suitable, stabilizing spiritual base. The church has, I believe, a role in creating that national heart or identity. The nation is in the process of becoming Christian and people are beginning to sense the inevitability of this change. Such an awareness will make them more inclined to flow with the tide and convert. In addition, Christianity is linked with the West which, in spite of its despised moral values is regarded with considerable favour at the present time. It would appear to me that Christianity is becoming a common touchstone for many and could become part of what constitutes a national identity. Certainly it is serving to bind people together.

Fourth, the church has within its teaching that balance for which the government is looking — a strong work ethic and sense of responsibility, high moral values and a call to love one's neighbour which can counteract the hard spirit of self-centredness and greed that is beginning to permeate society. For the Christian, service of God and nation, and faithfulness in one's occupation are vital, but there are higher loyalties and values that mute and control the blatant materialism.

Finally, with more than 35 per cent of the nation's school teachers being Christians, the church is having a vital role in the new moral and religious education courses. Most of these are first generation Christians and many eagerly volunteer to teach these new subjects. Even without active proselytizing, this can only advance the cause of Christianity.

And so in these many ways we see how God has been working to redeem the city of Singapore. He has ripened a great harvest.

## For discussion

While the church is generally in accord with national goals, there are areas where Christian values conflict with commonly held Singaporean values. What are these areas of divergence and how can the church deal with them in a constructive way?

# Chapter 5

# The City: Specific Characteristics

In the following two chapters we deal with a number of urban characteristics which are significant in the Singapore situation for the growth of the church. The government's ambitious programme of urban renewal and national development has drawn not only considerable praise but some heavy criticism as well from both sociologists and journalists. My purpose is not to defend the government but to facilitate a better understanding of the context of church growth in Singapore.

As I see it, many of the criticisms which are levelled at the Singapore programme are in fact criticisms of urban life in general as experienced all around the world. Urban living was a "given" for the national rulers of Singapore. The government neither caused it nor can reverse it because of the limited land available for development and because of the paramount need to industrialize the economy. Most of the features I have been able to identify in relation to Singapore society I find are general features of urban society. Of course they vary in intensity and significance from place to place, and during the course of discussing them I will attempt to indicate which are the most pivotal for Singapore itself and for church growth there.

Some sociological manifestations can influence society both positively and negatively at the same time. Further, things that from a societal point of view are pathological may actually constitute a positive force for church growth. It is important for church workers to be sensitive to these societal forces from both the communal and the church growth perspectives. Such sensitivity will make them better disciplers and shepherds.

We shall, in this chapter, discuss six features of urban life as they pertain to Singapore and the growth of the church.

## The Nature of City and Urbanism

Cities used to be defined in terms of size and levels of population concentration (density). But it is increasingly being recognized that city is primarily a distinctive way of life, a special form of human community exhibiting all the characteristics which we will discuss — specialization, heterogeneity, homogeneity, change, social mobility, secularity, anonymity, social pathology and so on. Each city has what McGavran calls its own "cultural personality" (1980:207), shaped by the general features of urban living plus the specifics — physical, economic, political, racial, military, religious, climatic — of its own unique locus and situation. The people of a particular city will have their own peculiar mindset and lifestyle which they will carry with them even when they are away from the city, in just the same way as a rural migrant brings his rural mindset with him to the city. There is a qualitative as well as a quantitative difference between rural and urban communities. The characteristic Singapore spirit is restless and relentless. It is, among other things, a product of Chinese determination, a seasonless climate, narrow geographical confines that never let the inhabitants escape from the all-pervading atmosphere of commercial and financial concerns, and a visionary, hard-driving leadership.

## The City as Navel and Specialist Centre

Cities are the centre of a large hinterland, and their focus is external. They influence their hinterland but are also vulnerable to changes within it. The Singaporean senses an acute vulnerability in regard to his hinterland. Having no rural surrounds of her own, Singapore's hinterland is Asia and, to a growing extent, the world. It is a hinterland she strives to influence but is more influenced by. Being dependent on imported water, food, fuel, building materials and industrial raw materials she is very sensitive to changes in her global hinterland. As a prime mover in ASEAN, she is constantly concerned to stabilize the militarily, politically, economically and religiously volatile condition of her neighbours.

When her economy depended on entrepot trade she was vulnerable but free to move her capital quickly to more promising fields when necessary. But now, with her capital necessarily tied up in specialist industries and her markets largely foreign, she is not only still vulnerable, but should the bottom drop out of an industry, there is no quick route to redeploying resources. This inescapable vulnerability is the source of a deep, underlying sense of insecurity which, in turn, creates a "go-getting" spirit in people who are forever striving and struggling to stay afloat, to achieve success, to grasp an elusive security. This spirit, so typical of Singapore Chinese, is evidenced in the aggressive evangelistic methods adopted by Singaporean Christians. And with their own kind, such aggressiveness is seemingly more effective than offensive, as it might well be elsewhere.

The same fate which pushed Singapore's horizons out past her own peoples and cultures and made her so vulnerable to what happens in other places has, at the same time, made her particularly open to the inflow of Christian influences as embodied in new organizations and methods.

Again, as the level of specialization and technical expertise rises, Singaporeans are becoming acknowledged leaders in many fields. This air of being leaders in Asia is reflected in the church in a growing sense of responsibility to be a missionary force to more needy surrounding countries. And this ministry is being undertaken with characteristic Singaporean enthusiasm, daring and efficiency. The young, Singapore-based Asia Evangelistic Fellowship now has over 80 Asian missionaries, and Operation Mobilization finds in Singapore a major recruiting ground, enlisting between 20 and 30 new workers from there every year. Short term mission teams are also a feature of many congregations.

## Heterogeneity and Homogeneity

We have already observed the potpourri of races, languages, cultures, religions, occupations and social classes that make up Singapore. Sociologists note that heterogeneity is one of the traits of the city. Cities are conglomerates of peoples, multicomplex societies, gatherings from the variegated hinterland of the metropolis.

But there are also within the city ethnic villages, homogeneous units with their own "consciousness of kind". Seldom is the city an amorphous mass. The British accentuated the pluralism of Singapore society by allowing migration from many parts. They also accentuated the natural tendency of urbanites to cluster into ethnic villages, by segregating ethnic communities into different quarters of the city, and even going to the extent of dividing the different groups somewhat artificially into occupational castes. The Hokkien people were designated merchants, the Hakkas, farmers, the Teochew, lighter and ferry runners, and the Cantonese, artisans (Hsieh 1978:186-192).

In view of this homogeneity, it is well to recall Donald McGavran's famed general guide to evangelism, that "men like to become Christians without crossing racial, social, linguistic, or class barriers" (1980:223). For people feel most at home with their own type and become Christians fastest when the least change of race or clan association is involved (McGavran 1980: 225). In Singapore we must certainly bear in mind that the Christian faith flcws well within pieces of the mosaic but tends to stop at ethnic and linguistic boundaries. However, having said that, there is, I believe, in Singapore a segment of the population which is what McGavran calls the "Urban Exception" to the Homogeneous Unit Principle approach to ministry.

*The Urban Exception.* Within the city there are varying degrees of melting together of parts of the mosaic. Commonly there is some production of biological and cultural hybrids. These are what Palen calls the cosmopolites — the singles, the intellectuals, who are attracted by newness and excitement and freely embrace anything that stimulates them, regardless of its traditional origin (1981:139).

The national government's aggressive promotion of ethnic and linguistic integration, with heavy socialization, has resulted in this urban exception being, I believe, a major segment of the population, especially among the younger generation. One of the hallmarks of being progressive, pro-government and elite in Singapore is to communicate in English and to adopt a certain Singaporean, professional lifestyle. There is a "new people" forming among the more highly educated segment of the mosaic. They are characteristically English speaking, have similar incomes, ideas, interests and types of housing. Class consciousness is high and ethnic consciousness low among these people. Ethnic out-marriage is on the increase among them and they join clubs and churches marked by these new values, regardless of race.

In most cities ethnically mixed churches do not grow rapidly because they are transgressing the Homogeneous Unit Principle (McGavran 180:244), but in Singapore, these "conglomerate churches", as McGavran calls them (1979:157), are the most rapidly growing because they are catering for a "new people", a new homogeneous unit that is developing with much government encouragement. The fact that the English-speaking churches of Singapore have been observed by sociologists as the most interethnic social institutions in the state, brings the church into good repute with the government.

**A Strategy for the Church.** The rapid growth of these "urban conglomerate" churches and the fact that the government is ensuring that a high proportion of the population will fall into the urban exception category over the next 10 to 15 years, indicates that this area should be a primary focus for church growth in the years immediately ahead. I would suggest that we should endeavour to form "urban conglomerates" at several class levels — for professionals, for lower middle income clerks, and for working class people. Government racial desegregation in housing, schooling and employment and its socialization programme is breaking down ethnic and linguistic barriers at all levels, leaving class stratification as the main homogeneous unit classification in the new society.

The concept of planning for "class" churches may sound shocking to some or even downright unchristian. But it should be understood that churches tend to develop naturally along either ethnic or class lines, or both. Given the choice, a new believer will generally gravitate to the congregation of people among whom he feels most socially secure. The motivation for forming" "class" churches is not snobbery or prejudice but a realization that people are more comfortable with their own kind. A working class person, for instance, may not be unwelcome in a professional church, but he will probably feel inferior, will not appreciate the intellectual Bible study nor mix easily with other members. No one congregation can satisfy the needs of everyone adequately. To be widely effective, a congregation will therefore focus primarily on one particular kind of people. The styles of ministry and worship, social activities and patterns of evangelism will be tailored accordingly.

Now that almost all Singaporeans receive English-medium education, English must be the language medium of these new "urban conglomerate" churches. However, I would suggest that these churches should work towards clustering around them, as part of their ministry, dialect congregations. There are still "ethnic villages" in Singapore, not geographically located but certainly existing as communities of people who will never be reached by the gospel unless it is through their own dialects. These are mostly the parents of the new younger set, and for that reason I believe they will be best served if the churches of the younger people provide dialect services to which they may confidently bring their parents. No single congregation will be able to make such provision for every dialect, but each could help in some way after taking a survey of the major family dialects from which their members derive. The official stress on Mandarin as a second language for the Chinese, means that the church should plan for more Mandarin congregations. However, as many of the older generation will never learn Mandarin, these people will need to be reached through their dialects.

Such a philosophy of ministry is totally in accord with government ethnic policies and also shows a concern for the older folk whom the government frequently laments are being neglected in the new society, particularly by the young. The church has here a special opportunity, for the genuine goal of its gospel and strategy is for a harmonious oneness without assimilation or domination. The spirit of the gospel is one of unity in diversity.

In that regard we can, with Harvey Cox, glory in the heterogeneity that provides richness, freedom and responsibility towards each other. And, at all times, great care should be exercised
to give place in church leadership to those non-Chinese in the
congregations who, because of their minority position in society,
will always tend to be a minority in the church as well.

## Change and Brokerage

There is general consensus among behavioural scientists that cities
are the locus of change. Robert Redfield described the city as
a centre of regular and rhythmic change that leads to the evo-
lution of culture. It is the source of cultural innovation, diffu-
sion and progress. Claude Fischer says that "non-traditionalism
and change are disproportionately spawned in urban environ-
ments" (Roberts 1981:88, 131). Roger Greenway describes the
city as "the very citadel of change".

There are many reasons why the city is oriented toward change:
its focus is external, it is the habitat of specialists who always
know something others do not, industry and modernity are part
of most cities and they are change related, and the city is the place
where strangers meet and ideas are exchanged.

Brokers are a feature of city life. They are the people who act
as bridges between distinct groups, associations and cultures,
they are those by whom ideas and values are passed from one to
another. Singapore has become a brokerage centre at many levels.
Traditionally she has been a city of transport brokers. As goods
have been transhipped between countries, ideas and values also
have been exchanged through these international dealers, and changes
have come to Singapore society. Today the government would
be the single most powerful broker and force for change. It is
ruthless and relentless in its drive to make the people for-
ward-looking and to be ever seeking more efficient and profitable
economic approaches. It deliberately searches abroad for the best
ideas in each field, sending its national scouts all over the world
to observe, study and learn. America is cultivated as a source
of technology, Japan is imitated in its systems of education and
business management, Israel is exploited for her military expertise, and so one could go on. The government has also led

the way among the financial brokers, using the Central Provident Fund as its main source of capital. It has rebuilt the city, developed an international financial centre, created a national airline and invested in new industries, in particular oil. It has been daring and creative, yet astute. The government has also led the way as a culture broker, changing the social face of the nation, developing new values and lifestyles without fully sacrificing the old.

This radical spirit of change, centred around the national ideology of utilitarianism, has been one of the forces for religious change. While the government has remained religiously nonpartisan, its utter pragmatism and demand that any way that does not conform with the values of efficiency and progress be rejected has inadvertently backlashed on traditional religion and created a positive attitude toward Christianity. The cosmology and values of Christianity appear to better fit the new worldview of technological man. Missionaries and church workers have been brokers of religion and culture and have been able to take advantage of the exceptional openness to change in modernizing, urban Singapore today.

But is this current openness to change a phenomenon that is likely to pass now that most of the populace has been comfortably housed and the city has joined the ranks of the developed nations? Geographical mobility will, in a few years, be exceptionally low for an urban centre. Once people have obtained their housing units, they will, in the main, perforce remain in one location for a long time because government housing is not freely marketable. However, the government is already beginning to remind the people that, for the sake of continued progress and prosperity, change must go on. It must be a permanent feature of Singapore society. With no natural resources, Singapore's life will always hang on a thread, the thread of the people's wit and industry. Inefficiency must continually be weeded out and more streamlined methods introduced or she will lose her competitive edge on the world markets. Such overall orientation to change, along with the related sense of national and personal insecurity, will, I believe, continue to make people open to religious change and keep them conscious of the need for some sort of religious under-girding. I see the context to be such that Singapore will continue to be receptive to the gospel for some years to come.

## Social Mobility

Besides the residential upheaval of the last 25 years, modernization and industrialization have also brought unprecedented social mobility. The sudden advent of modern companies, financial institutions and methods of business management has created a whole new generation of employment roles and relationships. The generation of the post-war baby boom was educated in English and trained for the new modernity. These young men and women walked right into these new jobs and have quickly risen up the new ladder of professional and business opportunity. No other generation will have quite the same opportunity for social mobility upward as have these young people who entered the job market in the period 1965-1980. There will continue to be a high level of intra-occupational mobility, but that is more of a horizontal movement and less significant socially.

There is a high level of correlation between those who received an English education and entered the professional job market and those who have embraced Christianity during the past 20 years. Most of these converts came from moderately poor homes but have risen so rapidly on the social scale that the church is now, to a high degree, composed of professional people. The national census of 1980 shows that, while Protestants constitute only 5.7 per cent of the population, yet 25.2 per cent of all tertiary educated persons are Protestants. At the other end of the scale, Protestants constitute only 2.8 per cent of those with no secondary education while in the overall population 65 per cent fall in that category. The church is very much professional and upper middle class.

From my understanding of the situation, the high social mobility among Christians is not due to the church growth phenomenon of "Redemption and Lift", at least not in its normal manifestations. There has undoubtedly been a degree of rise in social standing and level of income due to the embracing of a Christian work ethic and the transforming influence of Christ in the life.

But in the 1960s and 1970s there was, for one generation of young people, a set of happy coincidences. As we have already noted, large numbers of these, with benefit of English education and western curriculum, entered the job market during the first flush of modernization. They moved into the many new companies that were being established. As the companies expanded, so also did their jobs and salaries to the point where young adults in their 20s and 30s were already holding down important executive positions. It was the new values that came with English language and modernization that undermined the old values and left this generation in a spiritual vacuum. This, plus the aggressive evangelistic activities of the parachurch groups, led many of "the lucky generation" to convert. And so we have a generation of professional Christians who originated only a few short years ago from relatively poor homes.

But whatever the cause of this social lift among Christians, the effect remains the same. They are largely and perhaps increasingly cut off from the masses and, being oriented upward, find it extremely difficult to identify with people on the income level from which they came. This separation has very serious implications for the evangelization of the masses. The church has very few working class members and is showing little sign of breaking into that, the largest segment of the population. The only hope I see for the redemption of the masses is first, through the charismatics, as I have already mentioned, and secondly, through the few professionals who have the desire and capacity to cross social class barriers downwards. These need to be recruited and deployed as a missionary task force. From my observation, there are two groups in the church who show potential for being agents in forming a working class church. These are the social workers, school teachers and others in related occupations who work with such people, and some graduates who have recently returned from study overseas. Maybe, as far as the latter are concerned, their experience in more egalitarian societies has sensitized them to the needs of the poor, or maybe it is their own experience of being a little understood minority in a foreign society that has made them aware of the hurts of others. There are among these people those who are sufficiently caring and motivated. They must be found and banded into missionary units to form new working-class churches.

## Secularization

There is widespread feeling among social scientists that the city is a secularizing force. Robert Redfield saw the village as religious and the city as secular, and believed that money was the chief agent of secularization (1941:352-364). Louis Wirth attributes the growing secularization of the city to relativism and a tolerance of differences (1938:55). Gideon Sjoberg observes that in the village religion is diffused throughout all of life, while in the city large areas of life become exempt from religious injunctions. Rationalistic, secular philosophies replace religion. Financial structures which glorify man overshadow the cathedrals, and symbols of technology replace those of religion. God is no longer a shared presupposition, and society becomes permissisive rather than prescriptive.

I accept these findings in general, and note that secularism is growing in Singapore even faster than is the church. The 1980 census, which was the first to include statistics on religion, discovered that 10.3 per cent of the people were Christian and 13.2 per cent confessed themselves to be of no religion. Donald McGavran, as early as 1955, noted the collapse of animistic religions in the face of modern education, and predicted that most animists would convert to some other religion or to secularism within the next 30 years (1955:113). While his timetable needs to be somewhat extended, I do believe that his observation is very true of Singapore where traditional Chinese Religion is, at its core, basically animistic. Because this collapse of traditional religion is so central to the current experience of rapid church growth, I wish to investigate it, and the trend to secularization, in more detail.

*Observations About Change in Religion.* There are seven very pertinent facts about these current trends.

First, the great majority of those who change their religion are losing faith in traditional Chinese Religion and either becoming Christians or secularists. No other religion is gaining ground in Singapore.

Second, in a study done in 1970, it was found that the trend to secularism had a twist to it. Of the so-called secularists, 83 per cent were still interested in religion though not affiliated with any, 45 per cent claimed they had had experiences of the presence of some deity in their lives, and 67 per cent said they still sought help from some deity when they had a problem (Tamney 1970b:91-94). Evidently the problem is not that of pure secularism, but rather of a people who have lost faith in the particular form of religion in which they were reared. They are not negatively disposed towards religion as such and are mostly open to a new, more credible expression of it. Such an understanding of secularism in Singapore certainly throws a more rosy light on the evangelistic opportunity of the church. Most secularists, it would appear, have only become unaffiliated with religion because Christianity has failed to reach them with the truth.

Third, in my *Twelve Churches Study*, I found that 41.2 per cent of the Christians surveyed said that the primary reason for their becoming Christians was that they were seeking "the true religion". Their old religion had lost its credibility. So truth must be a central focus in our evangelism.

| Persons Aged 10 Years and Over by Religion and Highest Qualification | | | | | |
|---|---|---|---|---|---|
| | Total | Current Student | Primary or Below | Secondary | Tertiary |
| | (Per Cent) | | | | |
| Christianity | 10.3 | 11.9 | 6.0 | 22.9 | 35.8 |
| Catholic | (4.6) | (4.8) | (3.2) | ( 9.6) | (10.6) |
| Protestant | (5.7) | (7.1) | (2.8) | (13.3) | (25.2) |
| Buddhism | 26.7 | 24.8 | 28.1 | 24.4 | 16.1 |
| Taoism | 29.3 | 26.0 | 35.0 | 12.2 | 4.8 |
| Islam | 16.3 | 17.0 | 17.6 | 12.3 | 2.7 |
| Hinduism | 3.6 | 3.7 | 3.6 | 4.0 | 4.0 |
| No Religion | 13.8 | 16.6 | 9.3 | 23.3 | 35.2 |

(Sng and You 1982:19)

**Figure 2**

Fourth, statistics reveal that the breakdown of traditional Chinese Religion clearly correlates with levels of education. Most changes of religion take place in the age bracket of 14-16 years; in other words, during high school years. The intensive parachurch activity in tertiary institutions appears not to result in the same rate of conversions as is experienced through the parachurch groups in high schools.

Chinese Religion shows a marked collapse as adherents obtain higher levels of education. The more superstitious Taoist form is the most vulnerable. Those who drop out of Chinese Religion either become Christians or claim "No Religion". Other studies have revealed that Taoists with lower levels of education tend to convert to Catholicism rather than to Protestantism, possibly because of the more ritualistic style of worship with which they are more familiar. Herein lies a message for Protestants who would win the working-class. Protestants tend to gain most from the more highly educated and those with a slightly more philosophical Buddhist-type background.

Fifth, Christian schools and teachers have often been accused of undermining Chinese Religion, but such criticisms have been invalidated by several little-publicized studies. It was found that allegiance to Chinese Religion collapsed even more drastically in the Chinese-medium schools, where traditional values were strongly enforced, than in the English-medium schools. Ng Wan Weng discovered this and also observed that those who changed religions in Chinese schools seem to move from Chinese Religion to the secularist category, whereas those in English-speaking schools more commonly became Christians (Nyce 1970:43-44). This would suggest that those in Chinese-language schools would also be converting to Christianity in large numbers if the church had not failed to evangelize them. Almost all the parachurch and even church based evangelistic effort is being carried out through English-medium institutions. This is the greatest tragedy of Christian mission in Singapore. The only redeeming feature is that the government's recent decision to make English the primary medium of education for all Singaporeans is putting this largely untouched segment of national youth in the way of hearing the gospel.

Sixth, women traditionally stayed in the home and were thus unexposed to the new values, but the increased participation of women in education and in the workforce is exposing them also to modernization, with the result that females are now converting out of Chinese Religion at an even faster rate than males.

Seventh, Foo Meng Yeow discovered that science students convert to Christianity more readily than do arts students (Nyce 1970:43). One probable reason for this is that scientific studies are more powerful in undermining the presuppositions of the old world cosmologies. Another is that students of the humanities, exposed to the rationalistic philosophies and humanism of the West, find it more difficult to come to faith in Christ. As by far the majority of tertiary students are studying the sciences or business related subjects, this means that only a relatively few are hardened to the gospel through modern education.

In summary then, we can say that the sort of secularism currently predominating in Singapore is full of hope for Christianity. These people are not necessarily closed to the gospel nor resistant to it, though once they reach the labour force, it does appear that their level of concern to find a true religion diminishes somewhat. The figures above constitute an urgent call for new levels of evangelistic endeavour among this very receptive Chinese segment of the population. We stand in the midst of great opportunity. The fields are "ripe unto harvest" due to the collapse of the old worldview. James Wong, in a door-to-door survey, found that 22 per cent of people actually responded that they would like Christianity explained to them (Sng 1980b:270). To me that is remarkable.

## For Discussion

1. Is the ministry of your church geared for any particular kind of people? Is it adequately meeting their needs? What changes would you like to see made and why?
2. What styles of ministry, patterns of worship, evangelism and social activity would best reach working-class people? Remember that working class people are not less intelligent because they lack much formal schooling, but are less able to think abstractly. (A bus conductor or hawker might remember the exact change due to 20 customers at once, which is more than most university graduates could do.) Any meaningful expression of religion must therefore be more concrete and active.

# Chapter 6
# Reaching the City-dweller

The city dweller has a unique set of social needs which the church must address. The city also has its own characteristic channels of communication which the church must utilize for effective ministry. To this end, it is important to understand how people relate to each other in urban society.

## Anonymity
Many anthropologists, observing the very different types of relationships that exist in the city and in rural communities, have concluded that those of the city are impersonal and those of the village, personal. Robert Redfield (1957) characterized the city as a place of impersonality and anonymity. Louis Wirth, in similar vein, speaks of "the superficiality, the anonymity and the transitory character of urban social relations", observing that "physical contacts are close" for urban dwellers, but "social contacts are distant". He concludes that such physical closeness with social distance results in loneliness. The anonymity of city life releases individuals from social controls and results in urban crime and other anti-social phenomena (Roberts 1981:56-57; Wirth 1938: 1-24).

Undoubtedly industrialization has brought about some depersonalizing, dehumanizing effects. Village dwellers participate in person to person community while city dwellers cohabitate without relating, or relate only on a selected role basis (Tonna 1982:29). Because city people tend to be valued for what they can produce rather than for who they are, there is a serious loss of the sense of personal worth. They become mere statistics, cogs in the big machine, regimented and standardized. In such a society, the church will only be truly effective when it avoids the temptation to produce a canned, mass oriented message, and focuses attention on building genuine spiritual community and inter-personal relationships. Authentic Christianity will be recognized in the lived out reality of individual worth, not in institutionalized religion (Rooy 1979:198-199).

But there is also a positive aspect to all this. It must be recognized that urban anonymity, to the degree that it exists, does give people a freedom they never had in the tightly controlled, tradition bound village community, that is the freedom of individual choice, the freedom to accept the Christian way. When the individual is separated from his family and unknown by his next door neighbour, there is what Cox describes as a glorious liberty, full of new possibilities (1965:49).

## Individualism

Many urban sociologists see the village as more collective and the city as rather individualistic. Multiplex group relationships are often less and family ties weaker. Industrial society employs individuals and emphasizes individual responsibility, individual achievement, individual land and property ownership, and so on. As mentioned earlier, the Chinese always have had a strong streak of individualism, but in industrialized society even the family controls, which once modified that, are reduced.

The church should take advantage of this trend by emphasizing the value of the individual and personal responsibility for salvation. But this should be done without losing the sense of collectiveness which is also Christian and which the city dweller needs. People Movements can only take place to the extent that the church is able to build back into society a sense of collectiveness. The city dweller needs community and *koinonia*, but because of his individualism, extra effort will be required to ensure that he is adequately incorporated into the body, for individuals tend to hang loose.

## The Urban Basis of Relationship: Networks

While not wanting to wholly disavow earlier anthropological and sociological assessments of the city as the centre of anonymity and individualism, I would, with Eames and Goode (1977: 123) and others, hold to a more modified view of the situation.

While the traditional patterns of community and collectivity are not visible in the city, there are other patterns which emerge. The primary group relationship that characterizes rural society is largely replaced by secondary group relationships. In the primary group relationship, one collection of people interface at all levels of life. The individual fuses into this common whole so that individual identity and independence is considerably restricted by the social control of the group. The family and neighbourhood have a strong socializing influence. In urban society, the significance of family and neighbourhood is reduced, and people contact each other only in limited sectors of their life. There is a fragmentary nature to community which never results in consensus (Cooley 1966:280-283). A.F.C. Wallace, observing the pluralism of the city and the limited role-type relationships between individuals, described the urban world as a "mazeway". Networks rather than the single community group characterize life in the city.

In rural settings people have multiplex relationships. The same people relate to each other in a number of different capacities; they might relate as relatives, friends, workmates, worshippers and village officials. But in the urban centre, a simplex pattern of relationships predominates. People relate to different people in different settings, such as family, friends, occupations, religion, education, government, neighbours and recreation. The various circles of relationships may not overlap at all. These are specialized, limited spectrum relationships; in each one the individual fills one role. Eames and Goode say that "the city is the network of networks" (1977:242). In the city an individual can have network relationships to provide fully for all his social and psychological needs. However, it is an egocentric matter and a person might fail to build adequate networks and so face acute loneliness and suffer severe stress. Some societies help their people build networks better than do others (Eames and Goode 1977:157).

In a rural society the church does not usually need to provide community, but in the city the church needs to work hard to create a conducive environment in which people can develop relationship. In order for us to see the role the church should adopt in Singapore, we need to gain some understanding of the local network system. I propose to investigate what I consider to be the four most significant network systems in the city: neighbourhood, kinship, student and occupation. In my *Twelve Churches Study*, "friends" were found to be the single greatest influence in conversions and the primary reason for linking up with a particular church. "Friends" would refer to the operation of these various networks. "Student groups" rated second as a force for conversion and "family" third. Of course, some of those converted as students would also have referred to their conversion as being the result of friendships.

*Neighbourhood Networks.* Rachelle and Donald Warren describe neighbourhood in terms of both place and people. It is the sharing of a common geographical area of residence and reference. Neighbours are people you call on in times of need because of proximity of domicile, not because of intimacy. Neighbours are distinct from friends (1977:9-12).

The Chicago School of sociology believed that the neighbour dynamic dies in urban life and that with its death comes the end of community and personal warmth as well (Warren 1977:2). The national government of Singapore has felt a great responsibility for creating neighbourhood, especially in the light of its programme of relocating the mass of the population with the inevitable destruction of the old neighbourhoods. Numerous studies of degrees of neighbouring have been conducted in Singapore and various means have been utilized to develop healthy neighbourhoods. While these studies certainly do not fully agree as to the degree of neighbourhood that has developed in the new housing estates, there are a number of observations which can be safely made that might be profitably borne in mind by every church worker.

First, despite considerable external effort to build neighbouring, this network is quite weak in most government housing projects and is not the most fruitful network for evangelism. Yeung and Yeh discovered that 60 per cent of children play in their flats and never socialize with other children and the statistics for parent neighbouring are not dissimilar: 80 per cent of the parents socialize with others less than once a week, and most know only one or two neighbours (1975a:272-279; Chen and Tai 1977:78-93).

Second, many of the studies have idealized the old *kampong* (village) community, describing it as a close network of neighbouring, almost a primary group community situation (Walter 1978). In the light of that, they have lamented the "loss" of neighbourhood in the move to the new Housing Development Board (HDB) estates. But what I believe to be more perceptive studies have carefully gathered and compared statistics from both the old and the new locales. It has been surprising to find that levels of neighbouring are not, after all, vastly different. Those who were very sociable in the *kampong* soon made friends in the new housing estates, and those who had few friends before continue their pattern of isolation in the new location. Further, the children of sociable parents tend to have the most friends, while others are usually kept indoors to play (Yeung and Yeh 1975a: 272-279).

Third, neighbourhood takes time to build and surveys of the older HDB estates do indicate a growing level of neighbouring. In one survey, 92 per cent felt that the level of neighbouring developed with time (HDB 1982:18).

Fourth, early estates lacked the physical facilities necessary for neighbouring. Corridors and stairwells have been found to be impersonal space, not used for neighouring, whereas eating places, playgrounds, shops, clinics and community centres are more conducive to socializing. More enlightened concern for community is reflected in the better building designs of the newer estates (Eames and Goode 1977:166; Yeung and Yeh 1975a:262-264).

Fifth, few people seem to have adapted to vertical neighbouring. The floor barrier is a very solid one and this must be borne in mind when attempting to plant house churches (Hassan 1970:19). One survey revealed that 33 per cent had no social relations at all, 59 per cent had never contacted anyone in another block, while 72 per cent had never had contact with someone on another floor of their own housing block (Chang 1975:292).

Sixth, women, in particular housewives, do most of the neighbouring and so will be the key to planting estate-based house churches. Men commute to work and are away all the day while women tend to be forced into relationship with neighbours through their children and household crises.

Seventh, lower income people socialize more than do upper income groups. Lower income groups are less mobile and so more dependent on neighbours for social interaction. People with cars tend to visit family and friends in other social networks and they neighbour less (Eames and Goode 1977:147). The poor also tend to crowd more people into smaller flats. They leave their doors open for air and spill out into the corridors more than do more well-to-do flat dwellers (Walter 1978:238). Thus house churches will probably be a more viable means of evangelizing neighbourhoods in low income areas.

Eighth, cross-ethnic friendships are clearly on the increase and few of the people surveyed considered race to be a significant factor in choice of neighbours (Yeung and Yeh 1975a:271-272, 279).

Ninth, the government has worked hard to create neighbouring and has been disappointed at the results. However, I believe that the lack of neighbouring should not be seen in a negative light provided people have other adequate social networks. As observed earlier, neighbouring levels are seldom high in urban society and when people live in such close proximity, they need their privacy. When moving into new apartments people have usually purchased new furniture and equipment, and then, not knowing their neighbours, the locked door policy has developed. Also, with refrigerators, water and gas laid on, flats are self-contained and so women meet less frequently at the market and other old communal areas (Nyce 1970:62-64; Goh 1976:30-35). In fact, many people have expressed great relief at getting out of the *kampongs* where privacy was impossible and gossip rife (Walter 1978:241). In the relatively high-density living of the new housing estates, if home is not a private haven, people are likely to face "psychic overload" with resultant stress factors: mental illness and pathological reactions.

Tenth, the Chinese in particular have never had a high degree of relationship outside of their families and so we should not expect any sudden change in this respect now they are living in new housing estates. They tend to value household privacy and do not find neighbouring at all easy. Motivated by a strong sense of mission, Christians can, no doubt, bring themselves to neighbour for the sake of evangelism, but it will not be an easily created network.

**Kinship Network.** In Chinese society, the family, thought of in terms of the extended family rather than the nuclear family, has always stood as the primary and most powerful social unit. Often held together more by loyalty than love, it has nevertheless been the only strong social institution.

With the modernization of Singapore, and the rapid rate of change, a gap has grown between the generations that has weakened the family. People are tending to mix more with their peers in the new society. Urban relocation has also served to scatter the kinship groups. However, despite these weakening trends, the family is still a very influential network and most people visit family members more than friends on their days off. The wealthy tend to visit their parents more regularly, often daily, using them as baby sitters. The lower income groups tend to visit with family members who are located nearby regardless of the degree of closeness. However being less mobile they visit less frequently and tend to use their own older children as baby sitters.

A fairly recent study found that 20 per cent visit relatives daily and another 40 per cent visit at least once a week, usually Sunday. The women are usually most active in maintaining the kinship network, the mother/married daughter relationship being the closest of bonds. Males are more passive but nevertheless quite positive about family relationships, enjoying the regular visits. Among the middle class the strongest bonds are usually transgenerational. But among the working class, sibling solidarity is more marked, possibly because of a need to pool economic resources in order to survive. Most children also tend to relate more to their mother than to their father (Wong and Kuo 1979a: 17-35). An understanding of these patterns of relationship is vital for church workers who wish to work through kinship networks in evangelism.

One noticeable change resulting from urban relocation is the great increase in time spent with the nuclear family. Because of commuting to work and with television in the home, families tend to gather in the evening and at weekends and spend time together. When family members worked in the old family business there was little leisure time for doing things together (Yeung and Yeh 1975b:312-321).

The vast majority of the over two hundred thousand Christians in Singapore live in partially unredeemed homes. Most commonly, young Christians live in homes where parents and grandparents are unconverted. The potential for evangelism of all these contacts is mind boggling. It is not easy for young people to influence older family members for Christ. Their status in the family is low and, while 86.9 per cent of young people address their parents in dialect (Sng and You 1982:55), most converse in dialect very haltingly and have very little religious vocabulary. However, the church can teach its young people religious vocabulary in dialect, it can train them in witnessing to older people and can provide literature and tapes for dialect ministry. In my *Twelve Churches Study*, I found that 7.2 per cent of converts attributed their conversion to a family member. It can be done, and with concerted effort and careful training, the family networks could become a much more powerful channel for conversion. Donald McGavran speaks of conversion of kin groups as a web movement: "a somewhat disconnected long-drawn-out People Movement." We must work among Christians to create the vision for such a People Movement (1980:360). Again, in the words of McGavran, a pastor should say to himself,

> I must remember that whole families make strong, better Christians than lone rebels, and congregations built of inter-related persons have more endurance and communicative ability than those built of disparate individuals. Hence I shall seek to rebuild the web

inside the church .... I shall carry the good news from one section of the web to others and constantly teach that in Christ family webs are strong and family joys are greater than in the world (1980:362-363).

Even ten years ago young converts were not uncommonly treated harshly in the home, to the point of being beaten, locked up or starved. But one does not often hear of such incidents today. That people are turning to Christ is becoming accepted and this makes further conversions easier. Persecution, while a purifier of the church, is not the friend of evangelism.

**Student Networks.** In urban society people tend to relate more exclusively with their peers. Parachurch student groups have built their networks on the belief that one student can talk most easily with another.

As already noted, secondary school students are the most receptive segment of the community. They have lost faith in their traditional family religion and are very open to a more credible replacement. Influenced by western patterns of expression of affection, they are seeking warm relationships outside their homes, and Christian groups in schools have catered to this felt social need. Already hundreds of student groups meet weekly throughout Singapore, but this avenue of evangelism and nurture must be greatly expanded. The inspiration for and leadership of many school groups comes from Christian teachers. With some 35 per cent of the nation's teachers being Christians, we have a vast reservoir of leadership upon which to draw.

**Occupation Networks.** As previously noted, personal friendship is the single most powerful evangelistic force in the city. Such friendships are forged mostly in the educational institutions and places of work. Sng found that 25 per cent of Christians were involved in Christian occupational group meetings (Sng and You 1982:56), and certainly many more are openly identifying as Christians at their place of work and are striving to bring others to Christ. Such vitality in occupation networks augurs well for the future of the church. But here again, workers need to be encouraged to aim for even greater levels of influence among their colleagues. More professional Christian groups need to be formed, such as the already existing Christian Businessmen's and

Christian Lawyers' Associations, Christian Medical and Dental Fellowship, Graduates' Christian Fellowship and Teachers' Christian Fellowship. Besides being centres of nurture and fellowship, such groups should have a strong evangelistic emphasis.

*Evangelism Through Networks.* We have discussed various types of networks: neighbourhood, kinship, student and occupation. These networks are the key to human communication and evangelism in urban Singapore. A contagious Christian movement will only develop as it follows the lines of social networks. Charles Chaney insists that the gospel flows best along the lines of human relationship, and evangelism will be effective in proportion to its dependence on the establishment and cultivation of meaningful relationships (1982:168).

The church needs to take these networks seriously into account in its evangelistic strategy. Too often it has trained its members to witness to people whom they confront once and never see again. Little training is given by most churches for witnessing to friends and relatives in casual settings. The church should concentrate on using existing networks and bridges and should also help its people build those bridges of friendship through which they can then witness more effectively. Door to door evangelism, confronting strangers "cold turkey" with the gospel, brings very little fruit in Singapore. However, where Christians establish friendly relationships with neighbours, efforts to witness and plant churches in public housing estates are attended by more success. The foundational relationship as neighbour and fellow-inhabitant of a certain block of flats must be laid first. After that invitations to informal Christian home meetings will be met with a better response.

The dimension of this social aspect of conversion is seen in a study conducted by Bobby Sng among Christian university students. Of those surveyed, 60.9 per cent said they had been converted through friends and 13 per cent through kinship influences. In churches he surveyed the results were similar: 54.1 per cent said they were converted through friends and 20.2 per cent through kin. With older people the kinship relationship was more dominant. Of those aged 50 and above, 66.5 per cent said they had been converted through a family member (1980a:5-8).

Conversion has both a spiritual and a sociological dimension. Social influences are crucial for incorporating a person into a church. Lyle Schaller found, in his studies of American churches, that 60 to 90 per cent of people came into membership in their particular church because of the influence of a friend or relative (McGavran 1980:225). Sociologist John Clammer came to conclusions on the Singapore situation that concur with my own. People tend to go to the church of the person who led them to Christ. Geography and denomination play a very small part in choosing a church (1981:18-27). When people are relocated by the HDB, they tend to commute back to their old church or, if it is too far away, then frequently a group of friends will form a house church in the new residential vicinity. For friendship networks take on even greater importance when people have been newly uprooted.

Bearing in mind these dynamics for joining a church, it is important for churches to provide multilingual ministries so that the whole family, old and young, might be adequately catered for in the same church, if not in the same congregation.

*A People Movement Among the Networks.* According to Donald McGavran, "Cross-cultural evangelism limps until groups of related individuals start accepting Jesus as Lord and Saviour in a chain reaction". (1955:v).

> A People Movement results from the joint decision of a number of individuals all from the same people, which enables them to become Christians without social dislocation, while remaining in contact with their non-Christian relatives, thus enabling other groups of that people, across the years ... to come to similar decisions (1980:335).

I believe that in Singapore we have, at the present moment, a growing multifronted People Movement. There is certainly a People Movement going on among high school students. Sometimes groups of students decide in a "multi-individual, mutually interdependent" manner to become Christians, and at this time of high receptivity there are so many making such decisions that there is little sense of ostracism or alienation. At the university level, in occupational centres and in families, enough people are converting that Chinese everywhere know about it, and most people have a friend or relative who has converted to Christianity. Becoming a Christian in some student circles is seen almost as the enlightened thing to do; Christianity is becoming "our religion" to a sizeable segment of the population.

## Social Pathology in the City

Robert Schuller's philosophy of ministry is to "find a hurt and heal it" (1974:4). One could hardly do better than that as a guide to effective ministry. We turn now to isolate and examine those areas of life in which Singaporeans are hurting. These should then become to the church signposts pointing to areas where she needs to step in to minister healing, both to people individually and to society in general.

The symptoms of social pathology include rising levels of stress, divorce, suicide, mental illness, anomie, crime, juvenile delinquency, drug dependence, heart disease and cancer. To find the root cause of these ills, we must dig deeper. Certainly they are all on the increase in Singapore though they are not nearly as acute as in most huge cities. Despite the radical disruption of society through urban renewal, the level of social pathology has been kept remarkably low, probably due to the high degree of satisfaction felt by most people over their improved standard of living and the overall degree of safety in society.

*Symptoms of Social Pathology.* Between 1974 and 1983 divorces increased 342 per cent. Heart and hypersensitive diseases such as ulcers showed a rapid increase, replacing malaria and TB at the top of the list of killers. Suicides are on the increase, vandalism is just beginning to appear, and drug addiction among young people is a constant though not yet widespread problem. Anomie, social withdrawal, apathy, superficial relationships and insecurity have shown a marked increase in the last few years as people have begun to question the meaning of all this prosperity and pressure.

I wish to investigate four problem areas of society where there needs to be some social budgeting.

*The Physical Environment.* A lot of the early evaluative thinking, reflected in writings such as these of Riaz Hassan, expressed expectations of a significant increase in neuroses and psychoses as a result of the new high-rise way of life (Hassan 1977: 230-236). Because experiments showed that high density and high-rise living did produce sociologically negative symptoms in animals, it was anticipated that internal density (persons per apartment) coupled with external density (persons per acre) and elevation above the ground would produce psychological abnormalities (Chen 1978b:388-389).

In the early 1960s there was apprehension about living in such high buildings and there was some evidence of a rise in the worry index related to height above the ground (Hassan 1976: 240-265). But more recent research repeatedly shows that there is little clear relationship between density, elevation and social pathology (Chen and Tai 1977:66).

Eight useful observations might be gathered from research as to the effects of the physical environment of the new public housing on its inhabitants.

First, Chen, in a comparative study between Singapore and Hong Kong, concluded that density and height per se were not causative of social pathology. Human beings have a much greater capacity to adjust to new surroundings than do animals. Chen and others have concluded that social pathology is caused by the disruption of kinship and social networks through relocating people. Some people have continued contact with relatives and previous neighbours after moving, others have not and the withdrawal syndrome they evidence has had numerous pathological effects. The degree of stress, loneliness and anomie experienced through moving largely depends upon the temperament of the persons moved (Chen 1978b:390-391).

Second, the great majority of public flat dwellers are, in the main, well content with their new accommodation. For most, the new physical conditions are a vast improvement over the slums in which they once lived, and both internal and external density has been reduced (Nyce 1970:66-67; Yeh and Tan 1975: 220-223). Hassan, in an early study, found that 70 per cent of those surveyed felt they were better off in their new flats, and only 12 per cent regarded the move as in any way detrimental (1976:250).

Third, research has shown that the initial fears expressed by people in regard to living on higher floors is soon dispelled. In fact, many come to prefer the higher levels which are less noisy, less polluted, cooler, and free of flies and mosquitoes. In 1973, only 13.2 per cent said they would prefer to live above the ninth floor. In 1981, 31.7 per cent expressed that to be their preference (HDB 1982:18).

Fourth, the use of the lifts does constitute a mental barrier to going out and this results in some increased tension. When tensions get high in lower floor flats, people tend to go outside to cool down, but on higher floors, that way of escape seems too much trouble. Children living on higher floors are seldom allowed downstairs to play. This again adds to tension in the home and means that the child seldom plays with his peers or goes out of doors (Hassan 1977:230-236; Nyce 1970:64-66; Chen and Tai 1977:70-73).

Fifth, the predominance of "closed door", single nuclear families has resulted in the immediate family becoming more tightly knit than was the case formerly, when the identity of the nuclear family was lost in that of the extended family. Fathers tend to spend more time with their wives and children now than was customary in the past when they would have gone out with other men for their recreation (Nyce 1970:61, 64).

Sixth, the biggest cause of complaint is the noise level: children, funerals and television. Children tend to play a lot in the passages as they are not allowed downstairs. Dingy corridors and lack of security in stairwells and lifts are also a cause of complaint. New HDB designs have been improved in this regard by making corridors more attractive and turning stairwells into semi-private space that can be kept under surveillance by residents (Chen and Tai 1977:98-99).

Seventh, some complain of a lack of community and neighbouring which results in weak public security. Though the crime rate is quite low, still many are afraid to let their children out of doors and they keep their flats locked and barred. As mentioned earlier, there is a need for areas where people can socialize, but the government is finding that, even when care is taken to provide such areas, the level of community does not improve appreciably. People are self-contained in their flats and most tend to rely on family and friends rather than on neighbours for their social relationships (Chen and Tai 1977:71-73).

Finally, the government has worked towards building on only about 13 per cent of the land area, leaving extensive parklands for the people. But to this point, little use is made of this space. People prefer the small, highly used and more secure playground areas. Space is something Singaporeans have not been used to handling (Chen and Tai 1977:100).

**Income and Stress.** John Palen states that, worldwide, most crime is committed by young people from low income housing areas (1981:269). One piece of careful research has revealed this to be the case in Singapore. The three worst crime districts were studied. Two were in the early HDB flats, built specifically for people of low income (PD3, PD12), and a third was in a high density low income, private housing area which interfaced with a wealthy area and where racial groups lived in pockets but in close proximity to each other (PD14).

While all three areas were densely populated and had crowded, poor standard housing, that was not found to be the primary cause of the higher crime and delinquency levels, for the most crowded slum area of Singapore (PD1) was a very low crime area.

The chief cause of the troubles appears to stem from the frustration of being a "have not" in a society which emphasizes success and achievement and offers carrots to achievers and the stick to non-achievers. Poor home conditions make study at home difficult and result in early drop-outs from school. Where dwellings are particularly crowded, young people tend to gather in public places rather than in the home. In groups they then vent their frustrations by drug abuse, juvenile delinquency and crime. Being of limited education, they can never become achievers or live happily with government-endorsed values.

The few churches that work in these poor areas have had some considerable success in ministering to such crime-prone young people. They have salvaged many through their youth programmes and through provision of social relationship in a healthy environment. But few are ministering to low income people and the church needs to take seriously the missionary challenge to plant churches among the poor.

*Materialism and Insecurity.* In order to elevate Singapore to the status of a prosperous and developed nation, the government places considerable and constant pressure on the people to be competitive and to achieve economic progress. The people have bought heavily into this materialistic philosophy and have become prosperous. But there is a social price to pay, and many are beginning to ask the question, "For what purpose all this hard work and money?"

By use of the carrot and the stick, the government has stimulated individualism, egocentrism and human greed. Individual devotion to mammon has resulted in job-hopping after bigger salaries, with the consequent unstable state of the labour market causing a fall in productivity.

The schools have been ordered to promote the sciences and to inculcate in their students the new national values. The education system is producing economic digits and materialists, but the new values of materialism, individualism, competitiveness, expediency, efficiency and flexibility are creating a moral credibility gap that worries the government and all thinking people.

The new generation is not caring for the old, for this is not consistent with a philosophy of self-betterment and pragmatism. Elderly parents are increasingly regarded as an economic burden and a hindrance to achievement, and the young are unwilling to take responsibility for them. The new, successful elite is living ostentatiously and so accentuating for the poor their own lack of success. Parents pressurize their children to succeed at school, and themselves live and work under such pressure, that the build up of tension in their children causes anti-social behaviour, even to the point of some child suicides.

Koh Tai Ann calls for a moratorium on prosperity. Singapore must seek her soul. She must find a more enduring centre — a life enhancing, life justifying centre — instead of an economic centred, efficiency centred, meritocratic centred society. The city needs to develop heart and moral responsibility (1980:301-305).

The pursuit of material gain has brought an edgy frame of mind, a fall in moral standards and rising figures of nervous breakdowns, emotional disturbances, stomach ulcers, hypertension, heart diseases, strokes and cancer (Ho 1976b:120-127). There is a continuing sense of insecurity and urge to keep striving which leaves no alternative but to live under pressure. Many of the poor see little prospect of becoming successful, and this leads to frustration and resentment.

The government's recently reintroduced programme of moral and religious education in the schools is an effort to try and counter these manifestations of social pathology, but there needs to be a deeper change of heart and values if the rising tide of social ills is to be reversed.

The church enshrines those values which can restore heart to society and release people from their frenzied obsession with economic epicurianism. Her values are more compatible with modern life than are those of the feudalistic, traditional Chinese religions. But she must be prepared to be prophetic, even unpopular, in speaking out where values and priorities are espoused that undermine society.

*Anomie and Withdrawal.* It is the disruption of long term social relationships through urban renewal that has produced probably the most serious social pathology. The Chinese in particular do not find it easy to build relationships. Their traditional pattern of not showing emotion, especially not expressing affection, make it even more difficult for them to establish relationships that will satisfy their affective needs. Guy Lefrancois observes that, once a person's basic physical needs are met, psychological needs become a powerful force in his life. The needs for affection, belonging, achievement, acceptance, social recognition and self-esteem come to the fore (1972:304-305).

The new Singapore society has admirably met the physical needs of the people, but these psychological needs constitute a greater challenge and require more demanding solutions. The building of meaningful and satisfying networks and community is the paramount need of the new society, for anomie is on the increase. Hassan notes what he calls the Autonomy-withdrawal syndrome. People under stress are tending to withdraw into their own private worlds where they do not meet others. They become inward looking, impersonal, individualistic, apathetic and increasingly insecure. Any contacts they have with other people are superficial, conducted from behind a mask of self-sufficiency and disinterest (1976:260-261). Kenneth Leech, drawing on the research of Rollo May, calls this phenomenon the "schizoid society". People are out of touch with others, they avoid relationships, are unable to feel and empathize, are depersonalized, shut in on themselves, withdrawn and introverted (1980:97, 111-112).

The only answer to anomie, withdrawal and schizoid expressions is to be found in the building of community where people can be taught to express themselves spontaneously, where they can learn to give and receive affection and care, and where their own personal integrity and worth will be affirmed. In a depersonalizing society characterized by mass communication and production lines, the personal dimension must be restored and emphasized. And the church, of all social institutions, is best equipped to minister in this area. Christianity is a communal religion; fellowship and body life are of the essence of its being. In its gospel there is also adequate ultimate meaning and purpose to turn back the tide of anomie. One of the main reasons for the high level of conversion to Christ in Singapore is that the parachurch groups are providing the very community and sense of belonging for which young people search. But the church herself needs to work much more at developing this dynamic, for many young adults do not find these deep psychological needs being met in the church as they were met in their parachurch groups.

Singapore is a remarkable city and the government has a record of great achievement. But still there are unmet needs, needs for absolute moral values, for ultimate meaning, for relationship and community. Of all institutions, the church has the capacity to meet these needs. Of all religions, Christianity holds out a vision and hope for urban life. And Christianity, truly expressed, is the most relationship-oriented or societal of all religions. Reconciliation and community are the central issues of the gospel. The church can address these areas of acute social and personal need. It is within her power to transform an impersonal, mercenary city into a personal, warm-hearted community. This is the challenge and mandate that lies before the church in Singapore today.

We turn now to an analysis of statistics. To the more casual reader who does not relish statistics, we would suggest omitting chapter 7 and proceeding directly to chapter 8.

## For discussion

1.a    Look at the evangelistic programme of your church. Is it as effective as it might be? Do you have any ideas for its improvement?

1.b    Discuss the pros and cons of street, beach or door to door evangelism.

1.c    In view of what you have learned about networks in the city, what might your church do to plan for more effective outreach?

2.    What social ills do you perceive in society which are the result of urban living? Can the church do anything about them? Could your church do more to meet the needs of people so affected?

# Chapter 7
# Figures Speak

A careful analysis and interpretation of statistics can prove both revealing and useful. It will aid us in pinpointing factors which may be hindering or helping the life of the church. In the main we will draw from the *1980 National Census* and from my own *Twelve Churches Study* for relevant statistical data.

## The Church in Society

Christianity is the only religion that is making any significant number of converts, and most of these are people who are leaving Chinese Religion. The first century of the church was marked by slow growth, but that of the past thirty years has been rapid. At the present time I would estimate that Christianity and the category of No Religion are each gaining almost one per cent per annum of the total population.

Most recent Christian growth is Protestant. In 1971 there were more than twice as many Catholics as Protestants, but by 1980 we find Protestants far outnumbering Catholics (see Fig. 4). In those ten years the Catholics grew by 11,000 while the Protestants grew by nearly 74,000. Because of their sacramental approach, Catholics are not so free to use laity and house churches

| Per cent of Population Christian | | |
|---|---|---|
| Year | Per cent Christian | No. Churches |
| 1819 | — | — |
| 1840 | 0.38 | 3 |
| 1901 | 0.96 | 14 |
| 1940 | 0.59 | 46 |
| 1970 | 1.86e | 189 |
| 1978 | 8.00e | 261 |
| 1980 | 10.30 | 300 |
| 1984 | 12.00e | 320e |

(e = estimate)
(Pre-1978 figures = Protestants only)

**Figure 3**

in the way that Protestants do. Neither have they been very evangelistic, and most growth is biological rather than by conversion. In 1971, although their membership was so much greater, there were only 27 Catholic churches as compared to 189 Protestant churches.

Now, not only are the number of Protestant churches growing, but the size of each is increasing. In 1970 the churches averaged 186.8 members. By 1978 their average membership had risen to 301 (Sng 1979:8; Sng 1980b:304). The number of para-church and Christian organizations has grown from practically none in 1950 to several dozen now and their impact has been considerable. In 1970 there were 6 Christian bookstores in the city, but by 1982 there were 33.

## The Religions of Singapore
Over the last twenty years a large majority of so-called Buddhists and Taoists have been forsaking their traditional religion during secondary school years. They have moved, as we noted earlier, to Christianity or to No Religion, the latter gaining a slightly larger share due to the church's failure to evangelize among

Chinese-speaking students. Malays constitute 15 per cent of the population. No religion is gaining converts from among them: they remain solidly Muslim. It should be said, however, that there has been little attempt to win Malays, and now that their communities are being broken up through urban renewal, they may be much more open to conversions than has been presupposed. The considerable number of Malay inquirers at the Billy Graham Crusade in 1978 would indicate that there may be a fruitful mission field there waiting to be harvested. While 12.4 per cent of Indians are Christian, most are not first generation believers and little progress is being made in winning the Indian community to Christ. Of those Singaporeans who claim No Religion, 97 per cent are Chinese, and, as we have already observed, many of these are very open to the gospel. They are mostly the more highly educated Chinese. Of Christians, 79.1 per cent are Chinese.

## The Religions of Singapore

|  | Number | Percentage |
|---|---|---|
| Christianity | 203,517 | 10.3 |
| Catholic | ( 91,042) | (4.6) |
| Protestant | (112,475) | (5.7) |
| Buddhism | 529,140 | 26.7 |
| Taoism | 580,535 | 29.3 |
| Islam | 323,867 | 16.3 |
| Hinduism | 72,401 | 3.6 |
| Other Religions | 11,069 | 0.6 |
| No Religion | 261,433 | 13.2 |

(Khoo 1981b:3)

**Figure 4**

## Religion and Age

Christianity is fairly well represented in all age groups though predominantly among the young and English-educated. This indicates that a substantial number of teenage converts are holding their faith into adulthood despite frequent criticisms to the contrary.

The figures for the Buddhists and the Taoists are the reverse of Christianity, with the highest level of adherence being among those over 50 years of age. Catholics also have a higher age profile than do Protestants because they have not been evangelizing teenagers as aggressively as have the Protestants.

## Religion and Sex

Christianity registers a 10 to 25 per cent excess of females over males in every age group, the majority of these being converts from Chinese Religion (1980 census). The No Religion category has a predominance of males. Both males and females are deserting their traditional Chinese Religion, though females more so than males. While females tend to embrace Christianity, males tend rather to regard themselves as "free thinkers". The possible reason for this is that women are traditionally active in religious practice in the Chinese home and feel the need for a replacement of their old religion more than do males who traditionally take a more passive role in Chinese Religion. The church does have a significant problem here for, when she cannot find marriage partners for her young girls, she frequently loses them.

## Religion and Marital Status

In 1980, 50.3 per cent of Christians were single. This is a little higher than in other religions where Buddhists were 45.8 per cent single, Taoists 45.2 per cent and Muslims 49.6 per cent. Only those of No Religion had a greater predominance of singles. Not only do these figures reflect the overall youthful nature of the nation, but they also underline the fact that Christianity and secularism are spreading fastest among the youth (Sng and You 1982:16).

## Religion and Education

The correlation between religion and education was dealt with in the previous chapter in so far as the Chinese are concerned. Chinese Religion is losing ground and Christianity is gaining as the level of schooling rises. In the past, most Malays have not entered higher levels of training and have been isolated because of their more Koranic, less western style of education, although this is changing now. The Hindus have been little more open to conversion at higher levels of education than at lower levels. Possibly they have been held to their traditional values, at least on paper, by reason of their minority position in society and the need to preserve their identity.

## Religion and Literacy

Christianity had the highest proportion of adherents who claimed to be literate: Christianity 94.5 per cent, Buddhist 83.1 per cent, Taoist 75.5 per cent, Islam 86.7 per cent, Hinduism 89.8 per cent and No Religion 92.9 per cent.

The impact of Christianity amongst the English-educated is quite marked: 28.5 per cent of those literate only in English were Christians, while Christians comprised only 3.6 per cent of those literate only in Chinese. Both the church and parachurch organizations have failed to make any great impact in the Chinese-speaking community. There are indications, as previously cited, to suggest that these people are quite receptive, but that they have been neglected by the church.

## Religion and Occupation

As with education, we see a clustering of Christians in the upper stratas of the community. While 10.3 per cent of the total population were Christians in 1980, 28.0 per cent of those working as professional and technical persons and 24.0 per cent of those in administrative and managerial positions were Christians. A significant 17.4 per cent of those in clerical work were also Christians (Sng and You 1982:31).

However, in the blue collar, production industries, where 40.2 per cent of the workforce is found, only 4.0 per cent were Christians. The Christian presence in that large segment of the population is quite inadequate to evangelize the masses without help from missionary-minded Christians from the professional class.

## Religion and Housing

Public flats have been built to provide accommodation primarily for lower income families. In 1980, 68.0 per cent of Singaporeans lived in public housing estates but only 57.1 per cent of Christians lived there, and those who did were mostly to be found in the larger, more expensive units. Only 9.7 per cent of the population lived in private housing — bungalows, semi-detached and terraced homes — but, significantly, 27.6 per cent of Protestants were found to be living in this more affluent sector of the community.

What these figures underscore is the fact that Christians are occupationally and geographically divided from the masses, thus minimizing their capacity to witness to them in the course of everyday life. If the working class is going to be won for Christ, a special missionary effort is going to have to be made. To make matters worse, most churches and house churches are located in the private sector, separated off from the public housing estates where today 75 per cent of the population live. We will discuss this problem in chapter 12.

## Religious Convictions and Church Growth

In 1969, Joseph Tamney of the University of Singapore Sociology Department, conducted a study on religious convictions which, I believe, indicates one of the major reasons why Christianity is growing in Singapore. He researched under the classifications of Chinese Religionists, Muslims, Roman Catholics, Ecumenical Protestants, Evangelical Protestants, those Interested in Religion but Uncommitted and those Indifferent to or Hostile to Religion.

When asked about their convictions concerning the existence of God or some divine power, the Muslims scored highest with a 79 per cent assurance of the existence of God. They were followed by Evangelical Protestants, 72 per cent; Eumenical Protestants, 62 per cent; Catholics, 58 per cent; Chinese Religionists, 14 per cent; those Interested but Uncommitted, 13 per cent and the Indifferent or Hostile, 8 per cent.

The second question was, "Do you believe that everything that happens fits into a God's predetermined plan for the universe?" To this Evangelicals responded affirmatively, to the tune of 68 per cent; Muslims surprisingly, scored only 44 per cent; Catholics, 42 per cent; Eumenical Protestants, 40 per cent; Chinese Religionists, 15 per cent; the Interested but Uncommitted, 7 per cent and the Indifferent or Hostile, 2 per cent.

The respondents were then asked whether they had had a personal experience of the presence of their god or the spirits. Evangelical Protestants again scored the highest in their certainty and frequency of experience: 28 per cent said they "often" felt the presence of God; Muslims, 26 per cent; Catholics, 19 per cent; Ecumenical Protestants, only 12 per cent; the Interested but Uncommitted and the Indifferent or Hostile, each 1 per cent and Chinese Religionists, 0 per cent. One can see here why, in a highly pragmatic society, Evangelicals are growing the fastest, Muslims are holding their own and Chinese Religionists are losing ground rapidly. Evangelicals have strong convictions that their faith works and that their relationship with God is real and practical. It is surprising that, despite the interest of Chinese Religionists in the spirits, none of those surveyed could testify to having actually experienced the presence of the spirits on any regular basis; 54 per cent said they had once or twice had such experiences, 39 per cent said never.

When further questioned as to whether they sought the help of God or spirit beings when facing a problem, again Evangelicals gave the most positive response: 60 per cent always consulted the Lord; while the rates for others were, Ecumenical Protestants, 57 per cent; Catholics, 35 per cent; Muslims, 23 per cent; Interested but Uncommitted, 14 per cent and Chinese Religionists only 7 per cent. Again it is evident that Christians have the highest practical level of confidence in their God, and Chinese Religionists the least. Of those not committed to any religion, 67 per cent did, at times, consult God or some spirit being when they faced a problem, thus indicating that the level of receptivity or openness to religion was still quite high (Tamney 1976b).

These figures on levels of religious conviction, and the related growth or decline rates of each group, certainly affirm Dean Kelley's finding that conservative religion with its clear, firm convictions and strict discipline grows best (1972). While his conclusions related only to Protestantism, I believe they apply across the board of religion. Some further statistics throw some light on this phenomena of clear religious conviction and its effect on church growth.

## Denominational Growth Rates
## (Membership)

| | Founding date | DGR per cent | Dec. 1983 membership |
|---|---|---|---|
| Anglican (1973-1980) | 1826 | | |
| Total membership | | 79 | 8,181 |
| English-speaking | | 153 | |
| Chinese-speaking | | 17 | |
| Assemblies of God (1972-1981) | 1926 | 635 | 6,387 |
| Baptist (1971-1983) | 1937 | 114 | 3,890 |
| Bible-Presbyterian (1971-1983) | 1952 | 242 | 4,105 |
| Brethren (1971-1983) | 1864 | 74 | 4,156 |
| CNEC (1971-1983) | 1952 | 279 | 1,335 |
| Lutheran (1971-1983) | 1960 | 89 | 1,569 |
| Methodist (1973-1981) | 1885 | | |
| Total membership | | 77 | 16,060 |
| English-speaking | | 65 | |
| Chinese-speaking | | 93 | |
| Presbyterian (1971-1983) | 1881 | 76 | 9,116 |
| Independent (1971-1983) | | 167 | 10,025 |

**Figure 5**

## Denominational Distinctives and Church Growth

In 1979, Bobby Sng did a study of churches which he divided into two groups. Group A included the older denominations established last century — Anglican, Brethren, Methodist and Presbyterian. Group B was an assortment of churches formed since 1950 and mostly having clear, distinct emphases such as Pentecostalism or separatism, which marks them off as different from other churches. According to his figures, between 1970 and 1978 Group A experienced a DGR of 88.5 per cent, while the DGR of Group B was 155.8 per cent. Group B also showed a higher level of membership commitment and involvement in church activities than did Group A churches (1979:7-10).

My own study of denominational growth rates in 1982 resulted in similar conclusions (see Fig. 5). The figures given are again Decadal Growth Rates.

Part of the reason for the slow growth of the Anglicans, Methodists, Presbyterians and Lutherans is their high degree of institutionalization which we will discuss in the next chapter. Part of the problem is a lack of strict discipline, conservative doctrine and evangelistic emphasis.

## Congregational Studies

In my *Twelve Churches Study* (1982), which endeavoured to cover a balanced sample and included both regular attenders and members, I found the following data revealing.

*Sex.* 41.9 per cent were males and 58.1 per cent females.

*Marital Status.* 68.6 per cent were single. Some large churches had a very high proportion of singles, for instance Bartley Christian Church (CNEC), was as high as 87.9 per cent singles. Such a predominance of singles creates a special set of problems. For stability, the social and communal dimension of church life becomes crucial, and most churches are not serving their people well in this area. Mature leadership is lacking and attrition rates tend to be high, especially when the church cannot supply partners for all the girls.

*Age.* In those congregations surveyed, 69.5 per cent of people were between 15 and 29 years old, 31.4 per cent fell in the 20-24 year old bracket, while only 2.5 per cent were over the age of 60.

*Age of Conversion.* The average age of conversion was 14 years. with males converting at a slightly younger age than females (asserting their independence earlier perhaps). In all, 60 per cent were converted between ages 10 and 19 and after the age of 24 there was a rapid falling off in the number of conversions. Youth is clearly the period of peak receptivity and the church should exert every effort to reach young people in their teens without neglecting to go on to work for the conversion of whole families.

*Membership.* It was discovered that only 63.2 per cent of those attending had actually come into membership. This tallies with Sng's findings that as many as 35 per cent of Christians, and 51.9 per cent of the Christian students surveyed, have not been baptized. This is either because of parental objection or, in many cases, a lack of a sense of loyalty to the church or any conviction that baptism would be personally beneficial. Of those who had been Christians more than 5 years, a disconcerting 15 per cent still had not been baptized. Here is a matter of grave concern for the on going stability and growth of the church. Much teaching needs to be done in relation to this problem (Sng 1979; 1980a:6). The corporate nature of the Christian faith needs emphasis and it would probably help a great deal if parachurch organizations would demonstrate and inculcate in their members more loyalty to·the church of which, after all, they are a part.

*Length of Time a Christian.* The rapid rate of church growth, mostly through conversion, is evident in that 42 per cent of respondents had been Christians less than 5 years. This rapid growth is exciting but it does make plain the need for nurture because, at the present time, regular theological training facilities and evening Bible schools, large as they are, are not keeping pace with the need to equip shepherds for the flock. Many churches have never had the benefit of any trained leadership.

*Loyalty to a Church.* In my research, I found that 54.8 per cent of Christians had been attending their present church less than 3 years, the average being 2 years, and 59.2 per cent confessed to having moved around from one church to another. Only a small part of this interchurch mobility can be due to the governmental programme of urban relocation because, when people are settled in a church, they usually continue to commute to it even after they have been moved. But window-shopping is a way of life for urbanites and Singaporeans tend to window-shop for a church and do not settle until they have found one they like. From interviews conducted, I came to the conclusion that a great deal of this moving about is due to dissatisfaction with the quality of ministry and corporate life found in most churches. There is an urgent need for training of leaders in order to overcome this problem.

*Influences in Conversion.* In Singapore, Christianity is, for the most part, a religion of adoption rather than inheritance. Only 10.5 per cent came from Christian homes and many of those would be first generation Christian homes. The regular church programme is especially significant as a conversion factor, in particular the youth fellowships. In a separate survey, Bobby Sng found that 60.9 per cent attributed their conversion to friends other than family members (1980a:5). In the categories of Figure 6 many of the conversions could no doubt also have been attributed to friends. Kinship evangelism is clearly not as easy as peer group friendship evangelism. Sociologists observe that, in urban society, peer relationships grow stronger at the expense of intergenerational kinship relationships. Most conversions take place through the regular on-going work and witness of the church and Christians rather than through special crusades, and this is probably how it should be.

## Influences in Conversion

| | |
|---|---|
| Brought up in a Christian family | 10.5 per cent |
| Regular church programme | 36.1 per cent |
| Personal evangelism by family member | 7.2 per cent |
| Personal evangelism by a friend | 17.5 per cent |
| Student parachurch organizations | 13.3 per cent |
| Special evangelistic meetings | 5.7 per cent |
| Other | 9.7 per cent |

**Figure 6**

While parachurch groups are given credit for only 13.3 per cent of conversions, Sng found, in a student survey, that 58.4 per cent of Christian tertiary students were actively involved in such groups. In my questioning of church members generally, I discovered that 42 per cent had had such involvement during their student days. In my assessment of the situation, though these organizations profess to be primarily evangelistic in purpose, and though they undoubtedly prepare many for conversion whom the church harvests, their role in providing nurture, community and training is probably even more significant.

*Attraction to Christianity.* Respondents were asked what initially attracted them to Christianity because an understanding of felt needs is crucial if churches are to develop the most effective set of emphases. The answers given can be grouped into three categories.

| | |
|---|---|
| Looking for a true religion | 41.2 per cent |
| Attracted by the corporate life of Christianity | 35.4 per cent |
| Faced a crisis in my life | 18.4 per cent |

As already observed most converts are Chinese who have faced a credibility crisis in regard to their own traditional religion. The authenticity of Christianity and its consistency with modern scientific understanding, is a major issue with Chinese young people. They seek the truth. Second, we note once more the importance of expressing the social dimension of Christianity for the sake of lonely, disconnected young people. Third, ministry to people in crisis is obviously also a fruitful area of outreach. There are a few charismatic churches which are specializing in crisis ministry to great effect.

*Choice of a Church.* Figure 7 shows the reasons given for the respondents' choice of church. Again it is evident that friendship and the quality of ministry are the primary factors that bind people to a given church. The Sunday worship service is of fundamental importance because window-shopping worshippers usually measure a church by attending its window-front service, and if this is not inspiring and lacks the initial warmth of welcome, they will not return.

## Choice of a Church

| | |
|---|---|
| Grew up in the church | 6.1 per cent |
| Brought by a family member | 10.4 per cent |
| Brought by a friend | 23.4 per cent |
| Located near my home | 9.8 per cent |
| Church programme attractive | 37.7 per cent |
| People friendly | 8.9 per cent |

**Figure 7**

*Quality of Christian life.* The questions asked to probe this area revealed a high level of piety, diligence in personal devotion, and zeal in witness and service. All these are typical characteristics of first generation evangelical Christianity. 79.9 per cent said they prayed for more than 5 minutes every day, 65.9 per cent read their Bibles daily, 52.9 per cent had led another person to Christ, 41.5 per cent were involved in weekday fellowship groups, 79.5 per cent were involved weekly in some Christian meeting besides the worship service, while 45.9 per cent of all those surveyed had some serving role in the church. Such figures reveal a high degree of spiritual vitality and lay involvement. In this respect, the church in Singapore is in a healthy condition.

The statistics in this chapter give much reason for praise and encouragement for the future. Christians now number around 12 per-cent of the population and as they are, in the main, heavily involved in witness and lay ministry, we can expect even greater growth rates in the years immediately ahead. One of the main needs is for trained leaders who understand people's spiritual and social needs and whose high quality of ministry will be effective in this sophisticated city. The church badly needs graduates and highly-gifted young people who are willing to pay the price in prestige and income of taking up a Christian vocation. Graduates need to be inspired with a vision of what a Christian leader can accomplish in the growing of a church through quality ministry.

They need to be convinced that the Christian ministry can be one of the most challenging and fulfilling vocations in which a person can be engaged. It is not enough that families allow only their less talented sons to go into ministry while they continue to put their most able sons into medicine, law and management.

We come now to study the institutional factors in church growth. Our focus moves from the external contextual forces to those dynamics within the church which make or mar church growth.

## For discussion

1.   Is baptism and church membership really important? Compare the section on "Reasons for weak church loyalty" (page 39) with pages 118 and 119. Has the Bible anything to say on the subject? Discuss this question from the point of view of the individual and of the church.
2.   In view of the statistical evidence presented on pages 119-121 concerning influences in conversion, attraction to Christianity and choice of a particular church, what ought to be the major emphases of a church's ministry and programme?

# PART II

## Institutional Factors Influencing Church Growth

# Chapter 8
# Organizing for Growth: Structural Patterns

This chapter brings us to some nationwide internal workings of the church — national institutional factors — and their effect on church growth. In this regard we shall discuss denominational structures, church schools and kindergartens, interchurch crusades, parachurch organizations, Sunday schools, physical facilities and church size.

## Denominational Structures and Church Government

More heat than light has been generated in most discussions about forms of church structure and government. We do well to begin with a warning from Charles Kraft, that the *form* of church government is far more a cultural issue than it is a theological one. What God desires is not a single *form* of church government, absolutely right and valid for every society in every age, but, in each culture, the selection of that *form* which will best facilitate the smooth, effective and well-ordered operation of the church. Thus the *biblical function* will be expressed in *culturally effective forms* (1979:116-118).

*Hierarchical systems of church government.* We have observed in regard to Singapore that large denominations which operate on a synodal, diocesan or hierarchical system of government mostly show slow growth. Some church growth experts have concluded that this is a general principle of church growth. There are at least five reasons for this.

Peter Wagner, a firm believer in strong, directive leadership, is critical of synodal styles of government and for a very pragmatic reason. He has observed that in a hierarchical system, people are often awarded offices on the basis of seniority, influence, personality, political manipulation, prestige, rotation or all of these. He cites a principle developed by author Peter Lawrence, that "in a hierarchy every employee tends to rise to his level of incompetence". People who are successful in what they are doing are promoted to a "higher" task for which they may not be at all gifted (1979b:60-61).

Second, synodal systems rob congregations of responsibility and initiative. Parish priests are under the authority of the bishop and synodal committees. They are appointed with a specific job description to care for a particular congregation. This they may do faithfully but may not consider it their responsibility or right to start new churches or to launch pioneering projects. Promotion comes to those who play safe. This breeds mediocrity.

Third, synodal officials tend to be conservative and finance oriented. They are usually not visionary and adventurous, for that would be risky and would put added strain on the budget. In one of the minutes of the 1977 session of the Presbyterian Synod of Singapore, a pastor lamented that, during the last 22 years when many churches had been formed in Singapore and church growth had been of unprecedented proportions, Presbyterians had established no new churches and had made no major church extensions. Further, Presbyterians had not moved into any of the new government housing estates where 65 per cent of the population lived at that time. He called on the central executive of the Synod to be more aggressive (Presbyterian Church 1977:11).

Fourth, synodal executives usually lack the flexibility to adapt quickly to new ways and to take up new opportunities. Red tape and fear of taking chances holds them back.

Finally, Lyle Schaller has found that the ecumenics and politics at the executive level of denominations are generally associated with churches which are suffering loss of self esteem and credibility. They are usually introverted activities rather than evangelistic and they sap the church of its energy. Growing churches are marked more by intensity of belief, independence of spirit and missionary vision (1978:60-61).

*Congregational systems of church government.* Because of the weaknesses of the hierarchical system, it should not be assumed, therefore, that congregational church government will necessarily guarantee growth either. Peter Wagner again is quite outspoken about the kind of western, Christian thinking that, viewing everyone as equal in Christ, consequently insists on a democratic form of church government. Wagner is convinced that this thinking is both unbiblical and debilitating for larger churches. Biblical church leadership is based on spiritual gifts. A church leader who has the gift of faith should be allowed to lead and implement the vision the Lord has given him. The more boards and committees there are, the more the process of decision-making and implementation is slowed down, and the greater the potential for bickering and conflict (1979b:249-250).

Eddie Gibbs sees democratic church government as a system that neutralizes leadership initiative, and so frustrates leaders that they eventually resign themselves to accepting the status quo and operating according to policies of the "lowest common denominator" (1981:362-363).

There is a need for strong, visionary, flexible leadership, and normally this is best situated at the congregational level. Traditional Chinese leadership patterns did not follow democratic lines. There was a class of leaders whom the people followed. Western democratic patterns usually hinder rather than help the Asian church.

Having expressed this preference for strong leadership at the congregational level, I must hasten to add that visionary leadership at any level, if vested with authority, can be very effective in building the Kingdom, while lacklustre leadership will produce stagnation, whether it is at the synodal or at the congregational level. Two notable examples of this are evident in Singapore. In 1950, Rev Quek Kiok-Chiang and Dr Timothy Tow formed the first Bible Presbyterian Church. Their strong drive, convictions on doctrine and separation, mission and evangelism, have enabled them, from their position of executive power, to build, direct and discipline a denomination that in 32 years has grown to a membership of 4,105, with 27 congregations. It also has a Bible College, a home for the elderly, a book shop and an extensive missionary outreach.

Then again, when in 1966 Rev Chiu Ban It became the first Asian Anglican Bishop of Singapore, he inherited responsibility for a denomination which was numerically stagnant, partly liberal and certainly lacking in evangelistic fervour. He subsequently had a charismatic experience and, from his position of power, was able to turn the whole denomination around. The rate of growth increased, spiritual fervour showed a marked upsurge and, by 1982, all but one of the English-speaking congregations in Singapore had charismatic leadership. Dynamic executive leadership can be a great force for church growth, but history would indicate that a synodal system more often hinders rather than helps growth.

## Church Schools

The evangelistic impact of church schools has been much researched and debated. The research of Riaz Hassan led him to believe that church schools in Singapore resulted in many conversions to Christianity (1969). Catholic scholar Balhetchet came to the conclusion that Catholic schools had no decisive effect on pupils' concepts, motivation or practice (1976). M. Lau came to the opposite conclusion (Clammer 1981:35)!

A vast amount of money and manpower has been invested in church schools and, even today, some church planting projects are being held back because denominations require all their financial resources for school building projects. I believe we can draw five conclusions about the influence of church schools.

First, from early days they have been the handmaiden of the government, producing clerks with western skills and Christian values. The professionals have been heavily Christianized and remain so to this day.

Second, by their high standards and contribution to society, they have undermined early prejudice against Christianity.

Third, their heavy concentration on English education has been one of the reasons why Chinese-speaking churches have not grown. The latter have lacked trained leadership and an influx of converted youth.

Fourth, according to various studies, it would appear that during the period 1900-1930 the evangelistic impact of Protestant schools was considerable and planned. Between 1930 and 1950, however, there was much debate over whether church schools existed for education or evangelism. An influx of liberal missionaries and national teachers without spiritual concern, resulted in the schools having a reduced evangelistic impact. Since 1950, though, there has grown renewed evangelistic vision: Many principals are keen evangelicals, and school chapels and Religious Emphasis Weeks have taken on a more pointed evangelistic tone (Sng and You 1982:46-48). Since 1980, the government's concern to reintroduce religious instruction into the schools in order to stay the moral decay in society, has given principals and staff new freedom in presenting Christian truth.

Fifth, parachurch groups are having a profound impact upon the student bodies of both secular and church schools. I believe that the church is better served in the present era by concentrating on reaching young people through church and parachurch programmes which are much less demanding upon the church's financial resources than are schools. Further expansion of church schools, with its heavy capital outlay, would not be in the best interests of church growth.

## The Kindergarten Syndrome

Many churches operate kindergartens and play centres. But the question must be asked, "How do they fit into the church's priorities? For what purpose do they exist?" Most churches appear to operate their kindergartens as a service to the community. Allen Swanson found that, in Taiwan, declining churches operated kindergartens more than did growing churches and few churches used their kindergartens as bridges into the homes of unbelievers (1981:208-212). From my observation and discussion with pastors, I would feel that the same would be true of Singapore.

Given the land shortage in Singapore, churches do need to find weekday uses for their property in line with the government's concern not to have underutilized facilities. The church also should show concern for the needs of society and it is right in its motivation to serve the community through such means as kindergartens. But these operations must be co-ordinated with the church's primary responsibility to evangelize the people. Many pastors find their time and energy eaten up by administration, book keeping and finding staff for the kindergarten. As chaplains, they have regularly to speak to the small children, and most pastors find they are neither trained or gifted in this type of ministry. If churches are to continue to be active in running kindergartens, then these should be made part of the church's evangelistic endeavour and the numerous contacts should be seen as bridges into homes that already sense some gratitude to the church and possibly some obligation toward it. If the church is not prepared for that then the building should be leased to an independent kindergarten so that the church staff's energies are not diverted from their work of building the Kingdom.

## Interchurch Crusades

During the last 15 years, Singapore's Protestant churches have invested a great deal of energy and finance into nationwide evangelistic crusades. In 1969, there was the Grady Wilson Crusade with a total attendance of 46,000 and 2,092 commitments. Then came "Here's Life, Singapore", involving 7,000 lay workers, intensive home visitation and 9,104 commitments. The 1978 Billy Graham Crusade was the result of peak co-operation with 237 of Singapore's 265 Protestant churches participating and 15,000 official volunteers. From the first night the Stadium was filled to its 65,000 capacity and in all 20,000 decisions were recorded. In 1982 the charismatic churches combined to invite Paul Yonggi

Cho for a nationwide crusade. Denominations too have held frequent crusades of their own.

To what degree are these crusades an effective way of evangelizing the city?

Various studies have been conducted that indicate that such crusades may not be as effective as appears on the surface. Peter Wagner commented, in an article published by *Eternity* magazine (Sept. 1977), that fewer than 3 per cent of the half million who made commitments in the "Here's Life America" campaign could later be found in the church. In 1979 Wagner again expressed his doubts about the value of co-operative evangelistic efforts, stating that research indicates that "the more churches co-operate interdenominationally in evangelistic projects, the less effectively they evangelize." For co-operation tends to dilute the focus on the local church to which converts must be linked. It creates a gap problem in follow up, thus minimizing results in terms of church growth (1979a:64-72). He goes on to state that churches with rapid growth are those where members have a strong belief in their *own* church and recommend it with confidence to others. Such churches are very church-centred in their ministry, especially in evangelism. He cites Pentecostals as an example (Towns, Vaughan and Seifert 1981:258-259). Lyle Schaller also observes this phenomenon (Wagner 1979a:72-73).

In Singapore, Youth For Christ conducted a survey of the results of the Billy Graham Crusade 18 months afterwards (Sim 1980:36-38). Their findings were as follows:-

The Crusade certainly reached the unchurched; 62 per cent of all decisions were first time commitments. By contrast, it would appear that in the West such crusades mostly draw decisions from church people.

Second, 51 per cent of first time decisions never became involved in any follow up classes or church activities. They were lost to the church.

Third, indications from responding churches were that 10 per cent of converts could not be contacted, another 36 per cent said they were "too busy" or "not interested", 8 per cent denied any conversion, 13 per cent could not attend because of parental objection and 33 per cent preferred another church.

Fourth, of those who did begin follow up classes, only 22 per cent completed.

Finally, at the time of the survey, only 8 per cent of those who came to follow up classes had actually been baptized. So the level of incorporation into the church was very low indeed.

What conclusions may be drawn from these discoveries?

Despite the enthusiasm roused in these great organizational feats, there is a basic problem of a lack of ownership of converts. Churches tend to be better at following up those decisions made on their own turf, in their own congregational crusades. There is, in congregational crusades, a greater sense of accountability for follow up. Though the Billy Graham team trained follow up leaders for the churches and sent out the commitment cards, it is known that many churches failed to follow up those referred and never convened their follow up classes. The problem in most cases was not a lack of commitment to evangelism. Most churches are chronically short staffed, if they have any staff at all, and church workers, even without a Crusade, are fully occupied handling the growth they are already experiencing. With 20,000 commitments, the sheer numbers of referrals was overwhelming for many churches. For example, a certain church with one staff member received over 200 referrals in one week. As for the trained lay leaders, Singaporeans work long hours and there is a limit to how much follow up they are physically capable of doing.

Also, a crusade held on neutral ground such as a public stadium, makes it easy for people to attend but it establishes no link with the local churches. Around 88 per cent of those who came to the Billy Graham Crusade had never attended a church before. For them their first visit to a church would probably be even more traumatic than going forward at the Crusade.

And again, only 14 per cent of those referred had friends or relatives at the church to which they were referred. For the 14 per cent, undoubtedly these personal connections resulted in a better integration. Friendship evangelism takes into account the social dimension of conversion better than do crusades.

However, while the impact of these nationwide crusades is disappointing for evangelism and church growth, they have had a great role in bringing Christianity to public notice, making witnessing easier, training church workers and generally bringing the evangelistic mandate to the attention of the church. This is good so long as the church does not yield to the temptation to feel that crusades are doing the job for them.

## Parachurch Organizations

The large and very significant ministry of these organizations in Singapore has already been mentioned more than once. But, because there has been considerable friction between the student parachurch groups and the established church, there are some further issues that need to be discussed. Frequently churches have criticized the parachurch organizations for not building loyalty to the church, and sometimes there have been grounds for such criticisms.

The primary expressed purpose of most student parachurch groups is evangelism. However, they also have a significant social dimension in that they provide community for students. This is a valuable contribution in a socially disrupted society. Nurture and training is also a major aspect of their programmes. In actual fact, the Fellowship of Evangelical Students (FES) and Navigators put a very strong emphasis on nurture and fellowship while the Inter-Schools Christian Fellowship (ISCF), Campus Crusades for Christ (CCC) and Youth For Christ (YFC) are much more aggressively evangelistic. In my *Twelve Churches Study*, it was clear that the latter gained more converts. A study conducted by Goh Yue Yun showed that most conversions take place in high school years rather than at the tertiary level, despite the evangelistic efforts made there. He found that 80 per cent of FES members were converted before entering university, while the figure for CCC was 85 per cent (1981:69).

Goh also found that 93 per cent of FESers attended church regularly and only 76.9 per cent of CCCers did (1981:70). Sometimes too, parachurch groups, for example the Navigators, have demanded such a high degree of allegiance that this has tended to clash with church allegiance, throwing the two into competitive friction. Clearly the parachurch organizations do need to stress more the nature of the church and the importance of baptism and formal incorporation into the church.

This criticism notwithstanding, there are also some facts about parachurch members that the churches need to realize.

First, the parachurch organizations have been involved in ministry among the very receptive young in a way the churches have not. They are fulfilling a need and taking hold of an opportunity with which the churches have not adequately come to terms.

Second, the common criticism that parachurch groups steal the loyalty and labours of church members is not really true. In my *Twelve Churches Study*, I paid special attention to this problem and was surprised to find a clear alignment of loyalty to the channel through which people were converted, a very natural phenomenon. This loyalty was understandably most marked in the early stages of the Christian life. Those who were converted through a church tended to be baptized and come into membership quickly. But those converted through personal evangelism or through parachurch groups were slow to be baptized and become full members of a church. In one church, there was a situation where young people were being converted through the church youth group. These young people showed great loyalty to that group and its leaders but felt little obligation to attend the regular church worship services. Even children brought up in a church were slow to come into membership, maybe not feeling the kind of personal sense of gratitude that is felt by a first generation convert. The lesson seems to be, if a church wants loyal members, it must evangelize them itself.

Third, having raised questions about the loyalty of parachurch members to the church, I must hasten to add something else that I discovered. Most parachurch members are well trained in the Christian disciplines of devotion and service, and while they may be slow to come into actual membership in a church, those who attend church are, as a category, noticeably more devout (praying and reading their Bibles), more diligent and effective in Christian witness and more deeply involved in church life, especially in areas of service. The difference between those who were, or had been, parachurch members, and those who had not, was very marked in this respect. Thus churches that can attract parachurch members into their ranks will, contrary to much popular opinion, find themselves very well served.

Finally, young people have frequently been attracted to parachurch groups because of their intensive community experience. By comparison they often find themselves dissatisfied with the poor level of fellowship and social integration in the church. Partly as a result of this, and partly for other reasons, not a few student groups have decided to form their own churches rather than join an existing one.

## Sunday Schools

Postwar missionary efforts placed strong emphasis on Sunday schools, possibly because young children were the most reachable through the use of English. Many churches in Singapore began as Sunday schools, and the children converted in those Sunday schools of yesterday have become the leaders and elders of the church today.

While much fruit has come through this commonly used strategy, I would raise a caution. Peak receptivity to the gospel appears to be between the ages of 14 and 16. Sunday schools usually concentrate on younger children. Further, Sunday schools have a high loss rate among those making commitments because of parental objection. With limited resources, the church might more profitably focus attention primarily on youth work rather than Sunday schools as a channel for evangelistic outreach.

## Physical Facilities and Church Size

This will be a major subject in chapter 12, but a brief mention of this matter needs to be made in this discussion of structures. There is an acute shortage of land in Singapore and many people have advocated the house church as the most suitable model for local churches to follow. In fact, the house church model has frequently been idealized and upheld as the biblical pattern.

But church growth experts almost unanimously stress the importance of visibility and accessibility for churches in an urban setting. Frequently, visibility is the only way people will be able to find a church and be free to window-shop for a church to their liking as urban Christians like to do (Gibbs 1981:227). In Singapore, many churches meet in homes, hotel conference rooms, schools, rented halls and back alley buildings where they are very difficult to find. Insecure tenure also means that such churches are constantly on the move, and frustration with the church's inaccessibility results in loss of members.

Pastor Lim Kim-Toin vividly describes this all too common problem in terms of his own Presbyterian church. They meet beside a Christian school located on a narrow side street, sandwiched between tall, square buildings. They have no identifying tower or cross. Maps are given out with invitations but people still get lost. Those who do find the site then discover that there is no parking (1981:58-61).

Lyle Schaller underlines the importance of a large and beautiful sanctuary for church growth. According to his research, a stagnant church will grow quickly if it builds a new, attractive sanctuary (1978:58). I would confirm this as true in Singapore too.

Then there is the question of church size. The needs of older people can often be well catered for in a small, friendly church. But young people are looking for peer company and that in considerable numbers, and they are also very sensitive to the quality of ministry in a church. Large churches can have better facilities, better music, a team of leaders with diverse gifts and larger crowds of peers. In short, they can provide a better range of services and activities.

House churches are less than satisfactory at a number of levels, yet the path to producing megachurches is strewn with mountain-like obstacles such as land limits, government restrictions and real estate prices. Suggested solutions to this problem are proffered in chapter 12.

Having looked at the nationwide issues of church structures, schools, kindergartens, interchurch crusades, parachurch organizations and physical facilities, we now move on to discuss the growth of the church as it pertains to local congregational strategies and ministry.

## For discussion

1. Compare the advantages and disadvantages of interchurch, denominational and local church evangelistic campaigns. Where do you feel the emphasis should be?
2. What is the attitude of your church to parachurch agencies and personnel? How may a church gain maximum benefit from parachurch ministries?

# Chapter 9

# Dynamics of Congregational Growth

In a given context some congregations grow and others do not, and some congregations consistently grow faster than others. Obviously these growing churches are doing something right, providing something people want. Not that everything that grows is necessarily healthy. Cancer and cults grow. But a living organism that does not grow certainly has something wrong with it. As Dean Kelley says, there is "a certain inescapable, irreducible, quantifiable 'thereness' in an organization, which has some direct and discernable relation to its existence and success" (1972:16). Quality will have some manifest and measurable quantitative dimensions to it.

The task of this chapter is to identify at least some of the local institutional, intracongregational factors of church growth in the Singapore situation. We cannot hope to list them all, for each congregation will have its own unique set of growth factors which will only partially overlap with those of other congregations. Congregations cannot and must not all be the same, because people are not all the same. Any particular type of music, style of worship and pattern of programming will only suit a certain set of people from a particular socio-economic and educational background. Peter Wagner calls for each church. to be "fiercely pragmatic" in discerning what will be a blessing to the people among whom it has chosen to work, and to adjust its methods to meet their real needs and tastes (1981a:71-72).

## Intracongregational Growth Factors

Because each congregation is unique and is ministering to its own particular segment of the population, I cannot hope to produce a blueprint or complete list of local institutional growth factors that will cover all churches in Singapore. The bulk of this chapter is devoted to unwrapping some of those factors which my research has indicated are significantly helpful in many situations in Singapore. But, before doing that, I believe it may be helpful simply to list the institutional growth factors that different writers, from a variety of situations, have found to be important. The very number of factors described will serve to indicate the enormous range of possibilities there are. For instance, one researcher has identified 67 principles offered by McGavran, 51 by Wagner and 28 by Win Arn (Towns, Vaughan and Seifert 1981:109). The majority of these relate to the internal operation of the local church. My hope is that these lists and the more detailed discussion with its particular relation to Singapore will provide a "touchstone" and "trigger" to motivate and aid pastors in identifying the salient specifics for their own congregations.

We begin with some of the local institutional growth factors observed in different places by Donald McGavran, the father of the Church Growth Movement. They include: emphasis on house churches, use of lay leadership, observance of the Homogeneous Unit Principle, focus on responsive peoples and use of the language that will best reach them, obtaining adequate property, communicating an intense belief in Christ, providing a theological base for an egalitarian society (1980:322-330), planning and strategy geared to growth and church planting, indigenous leadership, good post-baptismal teaching (1980:162), a priority of evangelism over material support and education, and prayer for the salvation of the lost (Towns, Vaughan and Seifert 1981 : 111). Among the reasons McGavran gives for a lack of growth are: a maintenance mentality, ineffective methods, especially in regard to evangelism, setting pre-baptismal requirements which include spiritual maturing, ministers being so highly trained that they no longer communicate with their people, having church leaders who are not clear about church growth and who do not evaluate the work done, and leaders who accept gradualism and do not seek outside expert opinions when things go wrong.

*Peter Wagner's* catalogue of institutional growth factors includes items such as faith, strong leadership, laity mobilization, a large enough church to provide an adequate range of services, balance between celebration, congregation and cell, observance of the Homogeneous Unit Principle, effective evangelistic methods, the observance of biblical priorities, especially in relation to evangelism and social concern, and belief that God wants your church to grow (1984b), born-again membership, adequate and biblical teaching, nurture, a specific philosophy of ministry and its communication to the local community, personal piety and spiritual formation, spiritual gifts emphasis which involves mobilizing of the laity, fellowship, worship, missionary vision and a spiritual renewal emphasis. Wagner also has his own list of diseases which can cause a church to ail and might even prove fatal. They include "ethnikitis", old age and institutionalization, people-blindness, hypercooperativism or extensive interchurch cooperation, an excessive emphasis on *koinonia*, sociological strangulation, lukewarmness and a lack of the positive forces listed above (1979a).

*Lyle Schaller*, from his wide experience of church consulting, has documented a considerable library of advice for pastors and church leaders. A sample of the local institutional growth factors which he sees important in American churches includes: suitable church organization for growth, long-term pastorates, a corporate level of self-esteem among the members (they believe in their church), an adequate level of interpersonal relations, innovation rather than reform, a pastor who can adequately analyze a situation in his church and turn enemies into allies, must not adopt "enabler" leadership style ( see page 159 ), assimilation of new members, building in flexibility and change to counter tendencies towards institutionalization and stagnation, good music programmes, a wide choice of ministry styles and experience, a balanced range of skills in the staff-team, strongly evangelistic, ministering to felt needs, and reporting systems that measure the right things, calling for accountability and honest self-examination (1983).

*Robert Schuller* has the ministry of the megachurch particularly in mind in his suggestions for growth. His local institutional growth factors include accessibility, visibility, adequate parking, a wide range of services which suit the needs and timetables of everyone, visionary leadership, and adventurous budgeting. In a large church the programme should be exciting, helpful and well publicized. A church can destroy its growth potential by waiting for God to do it all, using ecclesiastical language, being boring and negative, relaxing in the glory of past successes, being small minded, losing spiritual direction, and preaching on controversial subjects (1974:19-46).

*Howard Snyder* lists a number of items that he considers to be barriers to church growth, among which are: spiritual disunity, immorality, false doctrine, rigid institutional structures, clergy-laity dichotomy, dependence on buildings, inflexible traditions, sterile worship patterns and non-use of spiritual gifts (1977: 119-121).

Coming to an Asian and Chinese situation, we find *Allen Swanson* enumerating local institutional growth factors for Taiwan. He found lay ministry and zeal to be the most powerful factor. Others included: strong leadership, a burden for evangelism, flexibility in methodology based on pragmatism, a strong pulpit ministry, goal setting, and freedom from traditional conservatism and resistance to change. He found many pastors to have a mindset that was uncreative and clinging to traditional patterns that were no longer relevant (1978:92, 96; 1981:216-241, 288).

Coming now specifically to *the Singapore situation,* I wish to discuss a variety of local institutional growth factors that, from my research, I perceive to be important. In this chapter we shall deal with those that relate generally to the worship service and to several other congregational issues. In the following, our focus will be on those that have to do particularly with church leadership and lay mobilization.

## Church Growth and the Worship Service

In an urban setting, churches that experience conversion growth will usually also experience transfer growth. And the majority who join a particular church will try it before committing themselves. In a rural setting there is frequently little choice of church, especially because family and clan loyalty stipulates which church a person may attend. But in the city there is much more freedom of individual choice. Churches are evaluated by "grapevine" reports, after which they are tasted by attendance at the worship service. If that is found to be attractive, then the potential church member may sample other aspects of the church's life. City Christians will window-shop and sample until they find the church that meets their tastes and expectations, and in Singapore there is evidence that many believers eventually become inactive because they never succeed in finding a church that suits them.

In a small church a visitor is noticed, and whether or not he returns depends to a great extent on the friendliness of the people. Poor quality music and preaching are likely to be overlooked if the new worshipper finds himself warmly accepted. In a large church he is unlikely to be socially integrated immediately and so the quality of the service will become correspondingly more determinative as to whether or not he returns. The assimilation factor will become important at a later stage. In fact, because many Christians always limit their church involvement to the Sunday service, this remains of paramount importance.

From my *Twelve Churches Study*, five general observations about the worship can be made. There was a marked correlation between the rating parishioners gave to the worship and preaching in their own church with the rate that church was growing. Low ratings by members invariably correlated with slow growth, whereas enthusiastic ratings were evident in rapidly growing churches. Probably this phenomenon reflects both the general attractiveness of the worship service and also the fact that when people are enthusiastic about their church, they invite friends.

It was also found that males and females showed no marked difference in the ratings they gave services, so the style or quality of the worship service is not responsible for the male-female imbalance found in most churches.

Third, the survey revealed little evident correlation between the ratings respondents gave their church for fellowship and the growth rate of the church. The quality of the worship and preaching seemed to dominate the picture. This was possibly because many churches provide very little beside their Sunday worship service for people to attend, and because many Christians find their weekday Christian involvement in parachurch organizations. Other evidence, however, indicates that the quality of fellowship is very important to Singaporean Christians.

Fourth, parishioners were asked to rate how helpful they found different aspects of church life, including worship and preaching. It was very noticeable that in some churches there was an atmosphere of excitement and fulfilment about every area of church life, while in others there was an evident depressed mentality. Charismatic churches showed a markedly higher level of enthusism in the responses of their people. Churches tend to have an atmosphere which is a conglomerate of a number of influences and it is a positive and expectant atmosphere that leaders must seek to build in their congregations. Parishioners generally felt that worship was the most important atmosphere-builder.

Finally, charismatic churches consistently rated worship as the most helpful part of their church life. Non-charismatic churches varied as to whether the worship or the preaching was rated most helpful.

## Worship

Peter Wagner reminds us that not everyone likes the same things. There are various philosophies and styles of worship. But whatever the style, there must be that essential ingredient that leaves worshippers feeling they have met God (1979a:109-110). No matter how solemn and dignified the worship, it must not be dull or boring. It must be alive; there must be an air of anticipation that something is going to happen, because God is present. Worshippers need to identify with what is going on up front, and the charismatics have reminded us that participation is a key to meaningful worship.

*The importance of music.* Probably the most universal key to the heart is music. Testimony that the right music can go a long way to creating that essential element of atmosphere comes from almost every stream of Christianity. Southern Baptist Jack Redford insists that it is music more than anything else which makes or breaks a service. He believes that, until high class musicians are found, a church will struggle. For that reason, a church should even give sacrificially in order to hire a musician, if that is the only way it can get one. Much thought and prayer needs to go into the preparation of music and worship, he says; there should be reverence, dignity, a sense of awe and yet, at the same time, there must be an attractiveness and warmth. "Joyless struggling through hackneyed old hymns" will never do. He also recognizes that the style of music used must fit the class of people who constitute the congregation. Professionals will desire more stately music and working class people more swing (1978:142, 152). Anglican vicar Eddie Gibbs believes that very few people can appreciate Bach and Stainer, hence churches need to update their music, replacing "goldy oldies" with a "new song" (1977:9).

Reformed scholar Calvin Chambers speaks approvingly of the change in music that has been brought about through the charismatic movement. He observes the use of more Scripture in song, a release from the egocentric nature of traditional hymns to focus on songs of worship in which God is addressed in the first person, a simpler, more popular style of music which is after effect rather than class. He welcomes the replacement of the sentimental, selfcentred gospel song with the music of true worship (1980:76-87). In fact, historians have observed that every renewal movement has been accompanied by a resurgence of a more popular style of music and this has been a major dynamic in the renewal. The message has sung its way into people's hearts (Latourette 1953:779, 827, 855-856, 867, 1265-1266, etc). David Watson comments on the immense popularity of Wesley's hymns and expresses his belief that the song was just as important as the preaching in the new evangelicalism (1978: 31).

Paul Yonggi Cho of Korea's Full Gospel Central Church, attended regularly by 350,000, says that choirs, organists, soloists and music directors "make or break a church". Cho attributes much of his congregation's phenomenal growth to good music, for "music is the language of our emotions, which is expressed through choral and congregational singing and through the use of instruments". Cho finds that prayerful music complements the message from the Word in three ways: (1) through music the church grows by praising God, (2) church growth comes as music edifies others, and (3) through music the church edifies itself (Global Church Growth 1983:xx:292).

In the same article reference is made to W. Austin Wilkerson of Houston's rapidly growing Evangelistic Temple. He too attributes much of their rapid growth to "an atmosphere created by God-anointed music which helps open man's heart to a God-awareness and worship". Well-planned music "will bring the believer into God-consciousness by its message," says Wilkerson. He also states that many new, immature Christians learn to pray and worship through the use of song, for it is music that ignites the responses within a person which develops into individual expressions of worship and praise (Global Church Growth 1983: xx:292). Betty Edwards, a secular art teacher, describes how music, lighting, seating arrangements, rhythm, physical movement and even private self-composed languages can serve to bring a mental shift from the analytical to the intuitive — that creative part of us that releases the emotions and inner-expression necessary for art (1979:197). This is, incidentally, the same part of us which needs to be activated for worship.

## Preaching and Teaching

Because of the limitations of space, we can deal only briefly with this second, but very important, aspect of the church service in its relation to growth. It is an aspect which also carries broader implications for the whole didactic function of the church.

Dan Baumann (1976) has a five-type classification for churches: the soul winning church, the classroom church, the life-situation church, the social action church and the general practitioner church, the last being a mix of the elements of the other specialty churches. "Classroom churches" are consumed with a passion to teach the Word from their pulpits and in their many Bible classes. Knowing the Word is regarded as the hallmark of spirituality. In my *Twelve Churches Study*, I observed that the Singapore churches where such an emphasis predominated tend to grow slowly. But of course, the quality of preaching and teaching makes a significant difference in the rates at which these classroom churches grow.

When we speak about the importance of biblical preaching, we mean more than imparting knowledge. G.L. Johnson, pastor of the fast growing People's Church Fresno, California, says that the key to church growth is preaching, but it must be lively preaching, with strong convictions, tailored to the congregation's needs. In regard to lively preaching, Johnson says,

> There are some churches that aren't growing because they do it in a dead way. You know — a monotonous, drawling sermon. If you've heard me preach, well, some people make fun of me, but I get loud, I laugh, I cry, I wave my arms, I stomp. It has spirit to it and life and I think people want this.

Johnson goes on to speak of the importance of the Word speaking to the needs of people It must be skilfully applied.

> When a family goes to church, and if they've got a daughter that's run away from home, or a son hung up on dope, or the man's lost his job, the woman's just learned she has breast cancer or home is like hell .... They want to know, "What does God have to say to my problem? What's the answer?" .... You've got to deal with a man's heart, his home, his problems — where he's hurting (Towns, Vaughan and Seifert 1981:59).

Preaching and teaching must be more than preaching truth for truth's sake. It must touch human need, be purposeful and elicit a response.

In many of the churches of Asia including Singapore, preaching is all too often dull, impoverished and anaemic. But Singaporeans belong to a crisp, fresh, vital new society, where time is money, and where communications are technically streamlined and sophisticated. They demand high quality. Seminaries, therefore, must train their students in the art of communication so that their message has zip and heart. Neither the old dictatorial pronouncement nor the wandering discourse will be tolerated.

Again, growing churches tend to have good preachers, and the pastor dominates the pulpit. I found in Singapore, as Swanson observed in Taiwan, that lay preaching tends to retard growth (1981:124-125). Sadly, because of the rapid growth of the church in Singapore, many congregations are wholly dependent on lay preachers. Communication is a skill requiring training and a high level of expertise. Preaching is a profession!

In my study, I found that men were more critical of poor preaching than were women, and, not surprisingly, the more highly educated people were more critical of preachers than others. This is a special problem in a city where the church is largely made up of professionals, and where pastors are frequently those who did not qualify for university entrance. There is an urgent need to create a new image of the pastor that will attract the most gifted from the Christian community into full-time service.

## Special Local Emphases

In the current Singapore context, the great need for *koinonia* or community in the life of the church would naturally come at the top of the list of necessary special emphases, but I wish to discuss this in chapter 11 on strategies for Singapore. The growth factors selected for discussion below are evangelism; mission; renewal; evangelical faith and conviction; celebration, congregation and cell; the cutback syndrome; and competition. These are only a handful of factors related to the local congregation, but I see them as most crucial in the Singapore situation.

## Evangelism

As long ago as 1927, Roland Allen described the close relationship between evangelism and church growth.

> We have seen again and again in the history of the Church that a Christianity which does not propagate itself languishes, if it does not perish .... Wherever the Spirit of Christ is, there is the Spirit which desires the conversion of the world to Christ (1960:41).

Jack Redford speaks from wide experience when he presses home the vital importance of evangelism for church growth. Because churches are born and grow through evangelism, he says, a virile, growing church will be fully geared to evangelism. In growing churches, he maintains, the message of evangelism is constantly kept before the church. It comes into every aspect of the church's life (1978:12-14, 145).

Peter Wagner heartily endorses Dean Kelley's conviction that the basic function of churches in society is to evangelize, and that churches function best when they are doing so (1981a:121).

One of the chief strengths of the church in Singapore is that many of its members are converted through and trained by parachurch evangelistic agencies and so they are both motivated and equipped to evangelize. Many of the problems faced by western churches in trying to move evangelism out of the church into the street is simply not a problem in Singapore's first generation churches. The evangelical gospel and strong conviction of Singapore Christians in a context of weak and waning confidence among other faiths has already been discussed.

But with so many new converts and so few trained in follow up and ongoing nurture, churches are failing to integrate many converts into the life of the church, and churches are also constantly tempted to give less priority to evangelism for a while in order to consolidate. Such a move has proved devastating for the churches that have done so. Not only is this course contrary to the will of God, but the church loses its head of steam and is usually unable to regain its evangelistic momentum again. Edification and evangelism are twin biblical priorities which must always run in tandem. The maturity and stability that comes from slowing down evangelism in order to consolidate is a stuffy stagnation. Converts who witness regularly are the most virile. Going out into the heat of the harvest is a maturing process; discipling is the expressway to maturity.

## Mission

We have already observed how Singapore is developing missionary agencies as it realizes a growing sense of responsibility for the evangelization of the surrounding region. Western mission societies are also finding Singapore an attractive recruiting ground. Giving to missions is becoming a major item on many church budgets as Christians realize that having received, it is now their turn to give. Southern Baptist David Finnell sees this missionary vision as crucial for the vitality of the church in Singapore. In a report to the Singapore Baptist Convention, he says,

> The church that loses missionary zeal and eschatological hope tends to become a church of the sanctuary rather than a church of the sign (miracle). Ceasing to be a driven pilgrim people, the church takes on more and more baggage, speaks of the Holy Spirit with great reservations, lacks enthusiasm and reluctantly gives credence to spiritual experience (1981:4).

The possibility of loss of fervour introduces us to our next growth-related subject.

## Renewal

In recent years many churches have been influenced by the writings of David Moberg, a sociologist of religion. Moberg studies church as a social institution and describes the life cycle of a church from birth, through virile youth, to aging and eventual death in the midst of formalism, indifference, obsolescence and red tape. From the midst of the youthful vitality and growth of the Singapore church, it is sad to read prophetic words of doom such as those of fundamentalist Baptist Elmer Towns. He studied the ten fastest growing churches in America and attributed their growth, not to organization, technique or method, but primarily to the "inner strength" of their youth, and he predicted that each of these "flaming witnesses for God" would eventually deteriorate and degenerate into liberal edifices. For "death is as inevitable to a church as to every newborn baby" (1973:154). Wagner has also written on disease, decay and death in the church (1979a). But he is not such a prophet of gloom; in fact, he encourages churches to be continually working to counteract the tendency toward institutionalization and decay, and he proposes remedies for the various common degenerative diseases.

The church in Singapore must not wait until it becomes deeply entangled in formalism and nominality before it seeks a cure. Now, even in its youth, there is a need to conduct renewal rites, not as an optional extra, but as an important part of the church's ministry. Those who have intellectually adopted the Christian faith and believe that is all there is, need to be helped to a place of personal encounter with God. Those who are spiritually vital must not be allowed to become lukewarm. Conventions and camp meetings are important "specials" in the life of the church as they can become channels through which Christians will be challenged to repentance and to new levels of commitment. In the enervating and unchanging rhythm of the tropics, these special religious events are even more crucial than they might be elsewhere as a means of counteracting spiritual drift and lethargy.

Renewal movements too can have a vital role, and throughout the history of the church they have come in many forms. But, undeniably, in our day and age it is the Pentecostal-charismatic movement that is the most significant renewal force, bringing new life and hope to the church universally. Donald McGavran observes that, when a church settles into such a deplorably low spiritual state that it cannot redisciple its nominal members, God sends in another branch of the church with a more authentic form of Christianity. At first, it is regarded as a sheep-stealing invader, but gradually, the older church is challenged by the more virile life of the new, and the Spirit of the new begins to permeate the old (Montgomery and McGavran 1980:166).

This has happened in Singapore. First came the classical Pentecostal denominations which were despised and often denigrated by the mainline churches. But, as the years have passed, the charismatic influence in those older churches has increased and with it new vitality and evangelistic fervour has risen. A study conducted in 1979 found that 37 out of 50 English-speaking churches had members involved in charismatic meetings (Sng 1979:10). Another study, in the same year, surveyed individual Christians and found that 70 per cent were aware of the charismatics and 36.4 per cent were personally involved (Sng 1980a: 11). Things have come a long way since then. Today almost all the Anglican clergy in English-speaking churches are charismatic and their congregations are increasingly following charismatic patterns of worship and small group meetings. Methodism too is experiencing growing charismatic impact, and a number of churches have had special waves of charismatic renewal which they call revival. This movement, with its emphasis on supernatural experiences and healing, is having a profound impact in revitalizing nominal Christians and is also bringing considerable conversion growth. For the Chinese are very power conscious and pragmatic; they want a religion that is intellectually credible, but they also demand a religion that is more than just informationalized truth; it must work. Further, Chinese tradition is supernaturalistic, not humanistic; divine encounter is expected.

## Evangelical Faith and Conviction

In *Understanding Church Growth and Decline*, Roof, Hoge, Dyble and Hadaway list a number of principles they have discovered in their study of American churches. Among them are these three:

> If contextual factors are equal, congregations will tend to grow if they strive to keep a clear Christian identity over against their surrounding culture.

> If contextual factors are equal, congregations will tend to grow if they maintain a clear sense of doctrinal truth, a clear system of meaning and value, intolerance to inner pluralism or dissent, and a high level of demand on members.

> If contextual factors are equal, congregations tend to grow if they maintain a conservative theological stance (1980:203).

These are very similar to the conclusions of Dean Kelley already mentioned. If they be true for America, they are even more so for Singapore where both society and government are more conservative, and where people embrace piety easily and thus find evangelical Christianity more palatable than liberalism. Despite the earlier presence of many liberal western missionaries in Singapore, liberalism has never gained a strong foothold. The clear, absolute doctrines and strong convictions of Christians have proved especially attractive during a period of loss of faith in traditional religion where beliefs were seldom clearly stated and reasons for practices often unclear. Meaning in traditional religion has been lost. Still further, there has been a strange attraction to the strict moral standards of Christianity, traditional religion being largely amoral. The high demand, high commitment churches are noticeably growing fast in Singapore today. There is, of course, another aspect to this. When strong conviction is coupled with Chinese individualism, it leads to much friction, factionalism and schism. However, unsavoury as this may be, it does, at the point of schism, usually stimulate further growth by the planting of yet another church in a very fertile field.

## Celebration, Congregation and Cell

By this three tier model Wagner describes his fourth vital sign of a healthy church. These are the three necessary dimensions of church life. Level one, *celebration*, is a festive, spirited worship service where the larger the crowd, the more joyous the occasion. The key to such a service is atmosphere and high quality presentation. Social interaction between individuals is not significant. In most cases this would be the Sunday worship service of a large church.

Level two, which we designate *congregation* (i.e. "to congregate"), is the structure that provides for general fellowship and social interaction. A group of 30 to 80 is fine, although if it consists of a predominance of single adults, the upper limit is to be preferred. This congregational or social dimension can be provided for in a small church or through a department of a larger church such as an adult Bible class or youth group.

Level three, the *cell*, resembles a family unit and provides for more intimate relationship and deeper person to person ministry. For the cell, 12 is preferable. 25 persons would be the upper limit (1984b).

Church leaders should be aware of these three dimensions

of religious and socioreligious life and endeavour to provide for them in one way or another. Obviously, the many house churches made up of single people can only provide the cell function effectively, and members of house churches have to go to Bible College evening classes, seminars and rallies to try and make friends and find the wider social interaction they need. Their worship experience also lacks the colour, flavour, richness and finish of the large celebrative experience. Many members of house churches and small churches go to large Christian rallies and attend large, lively churches on occasion to fill this lack in their own church experience; many others do not compensate and are spiritually the poorer for it.

At the other extreme, in many of Singapore's larger churches, the celebration is, in part, provided for, though the worship and preaching is frequently lacking in quality and is less than inspiring. But, because these large churches are understaffed and led by overworked and inexperienced leaders, there is often little infrastructure provided for congregation and cell. The worship service is the main event of church life, and so the members, especially the many singles, lack that social interaction, provided for in the congregational structure, which they so desperately need in lonely suburbia. They also fail to receive the personal nurture and care that can be supplied through the cell structure.

Small churches would benefit from being linked to a larger church or forming an association where they can gain the numbers necessary for occasional festive functions. Large churches need to work hard at developing the lower level structures that will make them more personal and caring, and will help overcome the perennial problem of properly assimilating new members.

Churches grow best when they provide a full-orbed ministry so that all the needs of their people are met. This involves the dimensions of celebration, congregation and cell, which will be expressed in a variety of activities to provide for the spiritual, social and psychological needs of the people. Over and above the spiritual meetings and social occasions, and depending on the particular context in which a church works, there may be need to provide also a nursery, a low cost medical clinic, a counselling service, tuition and other ministries. We have also noticed that churches will grow best where there is a multi-lingual ministry that caters for the whole family, old and young.

There are many more local institutional growth factors, but space will not allow discussion of them all. We conclude with a rather painful problem.

## The Cutback Syndrome and Competition

It is a common phenomenon in Singapore that, as churches grow and outgrow their accommodation in homes and rented facilities, they divide up into several groups but continue to regard themselves as one church. These groups usually get established in separate localities, develop their own communal spirit and witness in a local area. But invariably, when at last the church finds itself able to buy land and build, the intense pressure for funds tempts them to close down the satellite groups and centralize once more in order to be assured of the full financial support of satellite members. It is also done to save the rent on the satellite premises. This is the cutback syndrome. At this point several problems surface. When a satellite is closed down, an evangelistic opportunity is lost, for a point of witness in a non-Christian community is forfeited. This is a retreat action. Second, the recentralizing creates acute accommodation problems, causing some to pack their bags and move to less congested quarters. Third, a spirit of cameraderie and community has usually developed in the satellites which is lost in recentralizing. In a city so hungry for community, this is tragic. Finally, it is not unusual that the strong spirit of unity and community in the satellite causes its members to refuse to return to the mother congregation and so a painful split occurs. Though painful, this is, in terms of church growth, undoubtedly the best outcome.

With the Chinese independent spirit and tradition of running small, self-owned businesses, schisms are not uncommon and independent churches are a major dimension of Singapore church life. Many have lamented this fragmented state of the church, but, as mentioned in an earlier chapter, religion in Chinese experience has always been that way and people apparently think nothing of it. Denominations and church hierarchies, not independent churches, are the foreign concept. Competition between churches, if one wishes to describe it in those crude terms, is healthy not harmful. In the thinking of Charles Chaney, monopoly-like controls breed complacency, while many independent works lead to more aggressive witness and greater church growth (1982:65) A wide variety of churches provides more creativity and a greater possibility for cross-fertilization in the small Singapore community. And, in any case, with current high levels of receptivity, there are many more hungry fish in the pond than there are fishermen to catch them. We need more churches.

## For discussion

1.  In the light of what you have learned in this chapter on worship and preaching (pages 142-147), assess the strengths and weaknesses of the worship service in your church. List specific ways in which the quality of this service might be improved.
2.  Does your church meet both the religious and social needs of its members? Do you see the concept of celebration, congregation and cell as helpful in planning for a more full-orbed church experience? Suggest how these necessary functions might be fulfilled in your church.

# Chapter 10

# Keys to Success: Leadership and Lay Ministry

We now come to a discussion of those local institutional growth factors that relate to the vitally important areas of pastoral leadership and lay-mobilization. This chapter builds upon the preliminary observations made in chapter 3 on traditional patterns of leadership and authority and their implications for church growth (pages 50-54).

## Leadership and the Pastor

There is increasing consensus among growth oriented church leaders that leadership is the single most important growth determinant. For several years now, Peter Wagner's books have been making this point, and his latest release, *Leading Your Church to Growth*, argues "that if churches are going to maximize their growth potential, they need pastors who are strong leaders" (1984a:73). Robert Schuller is no less adamant. He says, "There is no substitute for dynamic, aggressive, positive, inspirational leadership! Almost without exception, the lack of success means the lack of effective leadership" (1974:48).

Towns, Vaughan and Seifert devote a chapter to "Aggressive leadership" and begin by stating that they have found strong leadership to be a consistent principle for building local churches. Southern Baptist, Wendell Belew comments,

> There is little growth of any kind taking place in churches in which the pastor has not played a key role ... In nearly every instance of exciting church growth, the pastor is the major motivator (Towns, Vaughan and Seifert 1981:207-208).

There is no doubt that this principle applies in Singapore. For instance, Our Saviour's Anglican Church and Prinsep Street Presbyterian Church were both old, long-plateaued congregations which, in the mid-1970s, received new pastors who had vision, dynamism and the gift of leadership. Consequently the growth graphs of both churches went into a steep climb. What do we mean by strong leadership? What does a pastor need to do and be in order to be a successful leader?

## Being a Leader

Field Marshall Montgomery said, "Leadership is the capacity and will to rally men and women to a common purpose, and the character which inspires confidence" (Hesselgrave:1980:355). *Leaders are those whom people choose to follow.* They are visionaries, possibility thinkers, motivators, inspirers, people with the gift of faith. They think ahead, plan for the future in terms of potential not problems, and gain ownership for their goals among a group of followers. They are the people who make things happen.

## A Leader is not Autocratic

Christian pastors, especially in cultures which have traditionally had autocratic leadership, tend to glory in giving authoritarian ultimatums: "Thus saith the Lord." Ted Engstrom insists that autocratic leadership is very destructive over the long-haul (1976: 73-75). It is *ruling* not *leading* and it begets *subjects*, not *followers*, whose own capacities and gifts are not drawn out and developed. Autocratic leadership is task-oriented, and power or force based. It has a low view of human nature and does not draw the bes out of people. There is a hierarchy attached to leadership, but a true leader does not depend upon the hierarchy for his authority; he wins it from below.

## A Leader is not Democratic

His winsome manner, willingness and ability to consult with others, and his sensitivity toward people, may make him seem democratic and egalitarian in approach. He may even confess his desire to seek the will and feeling of the people. But, when it is all said and done, the church is growing out of the pastor's vision and is directed towards his personal goals. Lyle Schaller is convinced that too much laity involvement in management, policy and strategy will seriously limit the growth potential of a church. Leadership and management, he insists, is a professional business. A leader must not even abdicate leadership to a fraternal committee of elders, though of course he must gain their ownership of his goals. Democratic style congregational government usually ends up implementing a colourless, tasteless and odourless programme, and even where a board of elders, rather than the rank and file, exercises strong control, one resister can hold back a whole programme. Furthermore, outsiders will be attracted to a church, not by participating democracy, but by strong, colourful and efficient leadership (1983:163).

## A Leader is not an Administrator

A leader is people oriented, an ideas man who inspires others to buy into his vision. Leadership is worked out through people. Administrators, on the other hand, are task oriented, implementers of the visions and goals of the leader (Schaller 1974: 174). The administrator is second in command, the manager, not the originator of the dream.

In a church, one man may have to fulfil the dual role of leader and administrator. Wagner observes that some people have a mix of leadership and administrative gifts. But if the administrative is allowed to dominate, the church will become maintenance minded rather than growth oriented (1984a:89). As a church grows, a leader should more and more delegate the administrative duties to others in order to leave himself free to be creative or, as Gibbs says, "free to roam on the growing edge and prepare for tomorrow as much as to preserve yesterday" (1981:342).

## Enablers are not Real Leaders

In Chinese society, a special leadership dilemma is faced. As already mentioned, clergy are still encumbered with a traditional poor public image and low self-image. Many churches are run by a board of elders who are older, conservative men, successful in business but often ill equipped spiritually and culturally to lay hold of the opportunities for outreach and growth in the new society. The gap between the present reality and the ideal of a strong, well trained, visionary, self-esteemed pastoral leadership is a veritable chasm. Some young pastors are beginning to lead strongly in young churches which are unhampered by older lay leaders, but frequently they are torn by a dilemma. Will they follow the old autocratic Chinese pattern and assert their authority, or is the servant, fellow-Christian style more biblical and more in tune with the modern, egalitarian spirit in society? Most believe the latter approach to be more Christian, but they are fearful of becoming a doormat if they step down among their people. Wagner has ably dealt with this problem in his latest book on leadership.

He quickly dispels the myth that the *servant* or *enabler* models of leadership are, in fact, the Christian ideal. Recognizing that God blesses many different styles of church leadership, he nevertheless goes on to demonstrate convincingly that, in practice, the gentle, non-aggressive enabler style of leadership has hindered rather than helped church growth. He shows that there is a valid alternative to the enabler model, an alternative that will cause churches to grow and yet still centre around a gift-based ministry. In this model the pastor is to be both a leader and *equipper*. He is to be responsible for receiving from the Lord the vision and goals for the church. In that he will stand alone. As equipper, he is then to go among his people to gain ownership for those goals and to train and equip the people to serve. His role and position in the church remains quite distinct from that of anyone else (1984a:73-88).

In the Chinese context, churches should be trained to work toward the implementation of this model. Pastors should be encouraged to lead strongly and to demonstrate that they have a vision from the Lord, the gifts to implement it and a special responsibility before God to make the crucial decisions relating to that dream. This does not deactivate the elders. The pastor should work toward elders being the implementers of the vision rather than the policy decision-makers. Elders should be helped to see that their involvement in actual key ministries will be much more fulfilling than if they are preoccupied with administrative and committee work. This will bring greater blessing to the church. I would suggest that, as the church grows and the administrative load becomes too heavy for the pastor-leader, an administrator be taken on to the staff rather than risking pastoral overload or a reversion to the old pattern of elder rule. We are in a period of transition from traditional to new, more effective patterns of leadership. Because of the industrializing and westernizing of society, many Singaporeans are already quite familiar with this new style of highly trained professional leadership based on talent and training rather than age.

## Who are Leaders?

Books on leadership can make depressing reading for young pastors, for they almost invariably insist that good leaders are born leaders and that very few people actually have the gifts of leadership. Sidney Rooy comments, "True leaders cannot be made, they can only be helped along the road" (1979:203). G.B. Vick, pastor of Temple Baptist Church, Detroit, has said, "Great men build great churches while average men serve average churches" (Towns 1982:99). Engstrom is convinced that few are born with the gift of leadership (1976:89). But, if one goes on to read the small print, there is still hope for the average pastor. Engstrom believes that people can change and he urges those aspiring to leadership to strive to learn the techniques and develop the personality traits of leadership. He insists that a person can change his personality somewhat through self-understanding and self-training. People can learn to become more personable, to handle criticism, failure and conflict (1976:89-93). Engstrom devotes several books to detailing what people can do to equip themselves for leadership. Elmer Towns suggests that young leaders study the great leaders and pattern their lives after them (1982:99). Every pastor can become a better leader than he currently is.

## Leading in Urbania

The urban world is pluralistic, complex and to many, quite confusing. One of the roles of a leader in urban society is to make sense out of the confusion and to explain that world to his followers, instructing them how to think and act in the midst of the seeming confusion. Thus, a leader must have the insight and capacity to be able to analyse life and society and to decide on suitable Christian responses. This procedure is quite noticeable in some of the bigger city churches. People tend to look to a pastor whose opinion they respect, and frequently accept his evaluations and interpretations of life and follow his directives almost blindly.

The way to maximum church growth in urban society is also complex, and well trained and capable pastoral leadership is essential if a church is not to blunder along on a trial and error basis.

## Leadership in Singapore

I wish to mention here just seven further observations relative to church leadership in Singapore.

First, with the rapid growth of the church, the supply of pastors has been quite inadequate. Many congregations have become familiar with the recent literature on gift based ministry and lay ministry, and some have even concluded that pastors are not necessary, and possibly even unbiblical. What has been said thus far should well establish the fact that there is a vital need for highly trained, professional leadership in the church, a leadership which supplements and gives direction to the diligent service of the laity. It must be clear that this new model, which gives proper place to the clergy, is in no way a return to the old pattern where the congregation employs a pastor to do all the work for them.

Second, in many Singapore churches, there is tension between the pastor and the lay leaders over the matter of authority. As is frequently the case, the lay leaders were in the saddle long before the pastor's arrival. In the early days, they were forced to shoulder the total responsibility for ministry and administration themselves. Later, on the advent of the pastor, they were happy to relinquish the work to him but not the reins. So, many a pastor burns up more energy in tussling with his elders for the right to lead and to use his gifts and training, than in anything else.

Third, it has been observed that pastors will attract to their churches people of their own age or younger. The Singapore church, which is predominantly young and increasingly manned by young pastors, is going to find it very difficult to reach the older generation or to minister effectively to them. Brainstorming consultations are needed to see if a way can be found out of this predicament.

Fourth, studies show that pastors mostly reach their own type of people. Those with a Christian background communicate best with young people from Christian families. First generation believers will be most effective in evangelizing the unchurched. There is emerging in Singapore the offspring of the first major flush of conversions in the 1950s and 1960s. There are very few pastors or Christians in Singapore who understand the mentality and problems of these second generation Christian young people who are now in the Sunday schools and beginning to reach their teens. Special attention must be given to developing an understanding of their needs.

Fifth, laity see the function of the pastor as shepherd of the flock, the one who is responsible for all the pastoral work. Given the acute shortage of pastoral staff and the physical impossibility of the pastor doing all the shepherding, a new image must be developed. One that views the pastor rather as *manager* or *foreman* might be better. Although the imagery is different, the good manager, like the eastern shepherd, will still be out front. His primary responsibility is to lead, plan and facilitate the programme and to oversee the workers. He will not be too proud to do the work where necessary, but he realizes that the whole operation will be more efficient and more widely effective if he does not try to be the whole team of workers himself. Lay workers then will acknowledge the pastor's special role in directing and advising and will themselves willingly do most of the visitation and basic pastoral ministry.

Sixth, when so many are first generation Christians, there are many lay pastors, and even trained pastors, who have little experience of church life. Many come into the ministry having never attended a Sunday school or seen a Christian wedding or funeral, and so one could go on. There is a great gap in practical experience here which probably can only adequately be filled by intensive training programmes and some experimentation. Patterns are inevitably being set for the future; we should ensure that they are good and culturally fitting ones.

Finally, I believe it is a myth that the working class can lead their own churches in a manner that they themselves will find really satisfying. They too live in a sophisticated society and tend to be passive participants in many professionally organized programmes. A poorly executed church life will leave them frustrated. It is noticeable that working class believers are congregating at some of the most professionally led churches in the city. They have a taste for excellence too. This means that there is need for some missionary minded professionals to plant churches among working class people where the ministry will not only be geared to their tastes, but attractively programmed.

We turn now to consider another important aspect of leadership.

## Philosophy of Ministry

Seminary students are trained to do things churches do, but they are not taught to strategize, to dream dreams, much less to contemplate a philosophy of ministry. As a seminary lecturer, I myself have tended to think in terms of there being one right formula or one set of activities that will make churches grow best. But I am coming to see that there is no one perfect combination. People, pastors and communities vary greatly in personality. Different people and peoples will benefit most by different styles of ministry, and no one church can hope to provide for the needs and tastes of everyone.

All churches have inadvertently developed their own peculiar emphases, but mostly this emphasis has evolved haphazardly. As a result emphases frequently do not suit the sort of community to which churches are attempting to minister, if in fact they have determined what sort of people they are trying to reach.

A church may direct its ministry to the immediate neighbourhood if it is a homogeneous unit. In that case its philosophy of ministry will include geographical delineation. It may aim for a particular ethnic and class group. It may aim to minister to some counter-culture group, or it may set itself to reach those in crisis situations. The possibilities are legion, but a church must narrow down its purpose and then clearly declare who it is catering for.

The name of the church should indicate the church's philosophy. If it is geographical, then the area in which it is to minister should be stated, such as Ang Mo Kio Methodist. If it has a special doctrinal emphasis or some unique practice, then that should be made clear, for instance, the Welsh Calvinistic Baptists, the Bible Presbyterian Church or Calvary Charismatic Fellowship.

Slogans are also useful. The pastor must establish a clear philosophy of ministry, gain its ownership with the church leaders and then share it with the church members and the community in which they hope to minister. We have previously mentioned Robert Schuller's catchy slogan, "Find a hurt and heal it." This emphasis constantly comes over in his church services, television programmes and advertising in the community. Everybody knows Garden Grove Community Church is the place to go if you have a problem or are hurting. The philosophy of ministry adopted by Jack Hayford of Van Nuys, California, is to be ever open to the ongoing leading of the Lord and to have a church that is a caring community. In line with that, the church is named "Church on the Way", and the sanctuary is called "The Living Room". Almost weekly, in services, the pastor stresses that the church must never become bound by tradition: its members are pilgrims, growing people, people on the way, never limiting what the Lord can go on doing with them. In a pluralistic society, specialization is necessary and, having established the area of speciality, a church must then gear all of its ministry to that purpose and constantly remind its people where its main thrust lies.

## Possibility Thinking

Churches have frequently become locked into a maintenance or caretaking programme, but of recent years, there have been numerous and timely calls to greater expectation. Robert Schuller rephrases the Scriptural concept, "According to your faith be it unto you," to read, "You've got to believe it before you'll see it" (1974:5). Much of the failure of the church to grow has been that it has lacked a vision of growth, expectation of blessing, and faith in God. It has had no eyes for the harvest. But let a church begin to pray, plan and believe, and there will be growth. Whether it be Schuller's "possibility thinking" or Wagner's "faith projections", the effect will be to lift people's sights and broaden the horizons of their faith so that they will reach out to take in more of the harvest in the name of the Lord. There must be strategies for growth in order to implement "faith projections", but the projection is the first step, for lack of faith has been the major cause of blockage. Our next point must be seen in that light.

## Church Growth Pastors

Dan Reeves of the Fuller Evangelistic Association suggests that one of the ways to help pastors develop a vision for growth is to get them exposed to the life of visionary churches. According to him, pastors will be small minded if there has been little exposure.

Wagner warns that there is a cost to pastoring a growing church. It is increasingly hard work, and pastors must want growth and be willing to pay the price before there will be any significant growth (1979a:24). Many pastors and elders are content and comfortable in their churches and not really interested in growth which is demanding and can be threatening when new staff and more elders join the team. Church growth will only come when it is wanted.

## Long term Pastorates

At the beginning of his ministry, Robert Schuller was advised by Raymond Lindquist of the First Presbyterian Church, Hollywood, "Never take a church unless you can envision spending your life there" (1974:73). Short term pastorates seriously inhibit growth. If pastors see their task as a mere holding action — preaching, baptizing, marrying, burying — then short term pastorates might be all right. But growth is not an overnight affair; growth takes time.

Lyle Schaller has found that the first year of a pastorate is taken up getting acquainted with people who are often grieving over the loss of the previous pastor. In the second year, the new pastor can begin to reveal his plans for the church. His most productive years do not begin until the fourth, fifth, or even sixth years.

Some churches in Singapore have frequent pastoral changes. Where this is the case, churches never experience the fully productive years of a man's ministry. Further, in a synodal system where pastors are regularly moved, parishioners get the feeling that they are transient beings and so expectations are low, and often people do not bother to develop a relationship with the pastor, nor do they take his plans seriously. In such churches pastoral patterns tend to be repetitive rather than progressive (Schaller 1978:53-55). It takes time to build a really great church. Big plans and faith projects take time to incubate, develop and implement, and the lay leaders will be unwilling to commit themselves to any significant visions of a pastor unless they are assured that he is going to stay with it through the rocky patches to the point of realization.

At the other end of the spectrum, Schaller also warns that a leader can stay too long, and this can be destructive both to himself and to the work. In Singapore pastors are often permanently linked to one congregation. Particularly in non-synodal churches, they are assigned for training by the church in which they grew up, they do their internship in their home church and then, on graduating, return there to minister. A pastor's early years of ministry are inevitably marred by some mistakes, the fruit of immaturity and inexperience. And a prophet is often without honour in his own country where he is remembered as one of the boys. There are times when both pastor and church would like a change. But in Singapore there are no channels for negotiating such changes, replacements are hard to find, churches have usually invested heavily in training the pastor, and pastoral moves are not the accepted thing. And so, if a pastor finds himself in an unhappy situation, his only choices are either to stay on in his troubled state or to exit into secular employment and so be lost to the ministry altogether. And in the Chinese culture great shame is attached to one who forsakes the call of God for secular employment. There is need for a good shame-free back door for pastors, a system whereby they can legitimately move to another church. Maybe a pastoral placement agency linked to the local Council of Churches or the Evangelical Alliance might help create an atmosphere where pastor mobility is more acceptable, and it could provide a channel whereby such moves could be negotiated.

Having discussed the important role of the pastor as leader, we now move on to discuss the mobilization of the laity for ministry.

## Laity-mobilization and Spiritual Gifts

It has been well established that churches where the pastor does all the work do not grow. Activating the laity in ministry is not only a biblical pattern and responsibility, it is also a secret of growth. Wagner lists liberating the laymen into service as one of the seven vital signs of a healthy church. He notes that in a small church of up to 200 members, the pastor can conceivably do all the work, but his church will cease to grow. The basis upon which a pastor should build a lay ministry is the Scriptural teaching on spiritual gifts. In fact, one of his high priority interests will be that of stimulating his church to operate according to a "gift theology", helping his people discover, develop and use their gifts (1979b:35-37). All Christians are gifted and so all should be serving in some capacity within the framework of the church's nurture and evangelistic programme.

Paul Yonggi Cho, senior pastor of the Full Gospel Church

in Seoul, Korea, attributes much of his church's amazing growth to the ministry of the laity. He has especially tapped what he calls the reservoir of "woman power". In a conservative, traditional society, where women do not take positions of leadership and power, he trained, authorized and released laywomen, not just into Sunday school teaching and menial roles, but into positions of leadership and congregational pastoring. He has drawn extensively on the commonly unemployed, larger half of the congregation. The pastor must be the *trainer*, equipping the saints for the work of the ministry (Eph. 4:12), if he would maximize the church's potential for growth. The Southern Baptists mobilize their laity through witness and Sunday school programmes. The charismatics involve laity in ministries of prayer and healing, prophecy and witness. Allen Swanson, in his research in Chinese Taiwan, concludes that there too, growing churches have all sorts of varying features, but one thing that marks them all is lay activity. People, according to Swanson, are looking for meaningful involvement, and the provision of such ensures that they stay.

In my own Singapore-based study of Chinese Christians, I discovered that males, in particular, found most fulfilment and spiritual blessing in active serving roles. More females felt sufficently fulfilled and blessed in passive participation in the activities of the church (not that they were unwilling to serve, or less active than males). But males expressed a felt need for challenge and active service in parachurch organizations and church programmes. They tended to become restless and dissatisfied if they could not find some active role in the life of the church (Hinton 1982).

Dean Kelley comes at this issue from an entirely different angle, but his conclusion correlates. He found that the higher the demand a movement makes on its followers, the greater will be its growth and overall impact. This is certainly very evident in the case of Campus Crusades for Christ, the Navigators and the Bible Presbyterian Church. Each is prospering remarkably and having considerable impact, and each makes high demands in terms of service and conformity to rigid standards and special beliefs.

*The "How" of Mobilization.* Reginald McDonough says that a leader cannot motivate a worker, but he can create a climate in which people will be motivated. In Singapore there is a tendency to regiment and drive the laity. McDonough warns that such autocratic patterns will backfire and bear bitter fruit. Leadership must be by inspiration, challenge, and encouragement, not by autocratic rule. As mentioned in an earlier chapter, the Chinese traditionally do not find it easy to express affection, appreciation and warmth toward each other. Church workers, both staff and lay, tend to hear from the church leaders only if something goes wrong. McDonough suggests that there are four keys to motivation: stability, teamwork, affirmation and challenge. It is in the area of teamwork and affirmation that Chinese church leaders need to work particularly hard.

Carl G. Kromminga, in an article "The Role of the Laity in Urban Evangelism", also makes this point. The clergy, he says, must train, support and encourage lay ministry. The feedback channels must be good and flowing with encouragement (1979: 139-143). Many clergy and elders fail to encourage their serving members. Sometimes they feel insecure and threatened, particularly if lay members are effective and popular. It is not uncommon for church leaders to undermine and thwart their best workers for this very reason. And while pastors have been trained themselves, they mostly do not know how to go about training others for service. They know how to teach information, but not how to help people to minister.

Lay workers often become disheartened, or are unwilling to take up ministry, because they are not adequately equipped to be effective in the task they are called upon to do. Many are trained to witness but few are trained in the art of follow-up, and long-term lay nurture, and so the attrition rate is high. Classroom type churches particularly keep their converts idle until they have built up a required amount of Bible knowledge, by which time they have lost both their initial fervour and the valuable opportunity of reaching their old circle of non-Christian friends.

In Singapore, Christian young people have often been well trained for lay ministry in parachurch groups. They are also eager to serve, but when they come into the church they find, all too often, no place to serve. Not a few pastors feel threatened by the confident manner of these newcomers and so coldshoulder them. This results in the immobilization and frustration of some of the best equipped and most devout lay people in their church.

In 1971, the Presbyterians had one missionary or national ordained worker for every 264 members. When one remembers that the attendance is greater than the membership and that evangelistic opportunities abound, this is gross understaffing. The situation was further aggravated by the fact that some of these staff were not even in pastoral work. In the same year, the Anglicans had one ordained person for every 302 communicants. Since 1971 the situation, Singapore-wide, has, if anything, worsened because the church is growing so fast. Lim Kim-Toin reports that, as of 1981, within Presbyterianism, there was only one pastor for every six congregations. Clearly the laity must be more fully and fruitfully utilized if the churches are to be adequately shepherded and the community fully discipled. The church must solve its laity unemployment problem.

Every church should study and diagram what percentage of its members are *attending* church activities other than Sunday worship. They should also calculate each year what percentage of their membership is involved in *serving*. This could, with advantage, be shown on a diagram such as Figure 8.

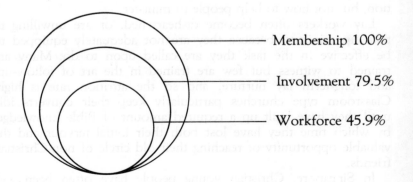

Membership 100%

Involvement 79.5%

Workforce 45.9%

**Figure 8      Laity Mobilization Profile**

In my *Twelve Churches Study*, I found that of the 3,500 persons surveyed, a heartening 79.5 per cent were involved in activities over and above Sunday worship (including parachurch activities), but only 45.9 per cent were active in any serving role in the church.

The Singapore church is, overall, strong in witness: 21.1 per cent witness at least once a month and a staggering 32.4 per cent have been the major influence in the conversion of at least one other person in the last two years, while an even higher 52.9 per cent have counselled someone for salvation (Hinton 1982). The church is well equipped for evangelism, but much more equipping needs to be done in the area of lay ministry for follow-up, nurture and general shepherding. Much of the church's supply of spiritual gifting in these areas still lies dormant, which is a tragedy in a day of such great opportunity and need.

In chapters 9 and 10 we have discussed an assortment of the more important local institutional growth factors in the Singapore situation. We now move on to the subject of strategy. First, in chapter 11, we deal with several of the thorniest problems of the Singapore church scene, suggesting solutions for implementation at the congregational level. Then, in chapter 12, we take a more macro view and suggest some directions for the development of the church as a whole.

### For discussion

1.  Consider the leadership patterns of your church. Where does the real authority lie? What advantages and disadvantages do you see in this present system?
2.  How can a church — lay leaders and ordinary members — help the pastor fulfil his God-given function and operate with maximum efficiency?
3.  In your estimation, is the proportion of lay members serving in your church high, average or low? Suggest ways in which more people can be given the opportunity to minister and be helped to exercise their spiritual gifts.

# PART III

## Strategies for Growing Churches

# Chapter 11
# Problem Solving:
# Dropouts, Sexual Imbalance, Poor Community

In this chapter we deal with three interrelated subjects that are major problems in the area of local institutional growth. They are those of membership attrition, the imbalance between males and females, and the need for more community in the church. I shall endeavour to be both diagnostic and prescriptive , for it is important to understand these intracongregational growth factors, and there is a crying need to overcome these problems because they so seriously retard growth.

## Dropouts

In chapter 3 we did discuss this problem in considerable depth and some statistics were provided which underline its seriousness in the Singapore church. The total loss to the church of converts who come in the front door and leave by the back is probably as high as one third of all converts. This means that for every three steps forward, the church takes one step back. It is a matter of urgency that something be done to stop this major drift. We shall see that this high rate of attrition is the result of a complexity of factors which I shall endeavour to unravel so that church leaders can perceive the nature of the problem they face. But in summary, one could say that most of the causes are to be found in two fields of neglect or failure: a failure to provide adequately for the social dimension of the Christian life, and a failure to make church life sufficiently relevant and attractive.

To gain some insight into the problem, 233 questionnaires were sent out to lapsed members from two churches. Many more could have been sent from these churches if total contact with those concerned had not been lost. Only 35 replies were received. This low response is probably indicative of apathy, resentment against the church and shame.

One gets the feeling that the largest number of persons missing from the churches studied have ceased to have any active Christian involvement. Then there are a considerable number who have tranferred to another church for a variety of reasons. One must also add to that transfer figure the large number of restless souls who over a long period wander from church to church and do not ever take root anywhere. The same causative factors lie behind many member and adherent transfers. The results of this survey compared with research done elsewhere provide the basis for the following discussion.

## Causes of Attrition

This list of causes is doubtless incomplete but it is adequate to portray the nature of the problem.

I begin by briefly recapitulating on some of the major causative factors associated with Chinese tradition and traditional religions as observed in chapter 3. Christianity has all too often been presented as a religion of the textbook and the head. It has been too cerebral and has lacked adequate practical outworkings in the dimensions of a tranformed life and encounter with God, as one observes it in the New Testament. As a result many a pragmatic Chinese has lost interest. For the Chinese, religion has been problem oriented. When the crisis is over or the loneliness passes, there is a tendency to become religiously inactive again. Linked with this utilitarian approach to religion is the tradition of diffused rather than institutional religion. There is a lack of loyalty to a particular religious institution and this has carried over into the church where converts, while attending, are slow to cast in their lot as full members with a particular congregation. Modern Chinese young people are hungry for affection and community but traditional patterns make the expression of warmth, love and concern difficult. So converts coming to the church for social reasons, become disillusioned with the lack of community.

We go on now to make some further observations.

1. *Boredom.* According to Eddie Gibbs, "today more people are lost from the church through sheer boredom than from any other cause." He quotes A.W. Tozer's description of the usual run of church service, in the obvious expectation that his readers will know what he means.

> The worshipper sits in a state of suspended mentation; a kind of dreamy numbness creeps upon him; he hears words but they do not register; he cannot relate them to anything on his own life-level. He is conscious of having entered a kind of half-world; his mind surrenders itself to a more or less pleasant mood which passes with the benediction leaving no trace behind. It does not affect anything in his everyday life. He is aware of no power, no presence, no spiritual reality. There is simply nothing in his experience corresponding to the things which he heard from the pulpit or sang in the hymns (Gibbs 1977:7).

The poor standard of preaching and poorer quality of worship in many churches is certainly a cause of attrition in Singapore. Sng refers to it as such (Sng and You 1982:52) and one often hears comments reflecting boredom.

Gibbs also refers to the strong centrifugal evangelistic emphasis of the church today, and compares it to the centripetal element of evangelism in the New Testament church. We go out and aggressively evangelize, but when converts come to the church they find little that is attractive or meets their needs. In the first century the church had a strong, attractive force about it (1981:

41-42). There people met God, worship was alive and meaningful, prayer was an avid encounter and signs and wonders drew people to faith. The church today needs to rediscover that magnetic power.

Urban young people are very demanding. They are aggressive, achievement oriented, and are struggling and scratching their way to the top. Urbanized personalities are characteristically tough, callous, insensitive and impatient. At work they set high standards and spurn the mediocre, and when they come to church, they do not change. They expect church leaders to be excellers.

2. *Lack of relevance.* Lyle Schaller makes another point that relates to this. He finds two classes of people in the church: those committed to the contemporary goals of the church and those committed to its heritage. He finds that the attrition rate is usually much higher among the former (1974:53-59). In Singapore, with the great majority of Christians being recent converts, almost the entire congregation is there because of contemporary goals. If they find that the church is not living up to its confessed goals, or that the church is not meeting their present personal needs, they are quick to abandon ship. Of course it is far from adequate motivation for people to stay in a church simply because of traditional or family links with the church but such a situation is much more stable than the one we face at the moment. Ministry must be executed at a high standard, services must be relevant and brisk or people will be lost to the church, and, even worse, lost to Christian involvement altogether.

3. *Worldly ambition.* The greatest attrition rate appears to be in the age category 25-39 years. Allen Swanson found the same to be true of Chinese in Taiwan (1981:210). This is the period when ambitions related to careers sidetrack many, especially fellows. Many, when asked why they no longer attend church, reply "too busy!"

4. *Opposition.* As mentioned earlier, persecution in the home was a common experience for new converts in the past. Such pressures are lessening but are still a significant cause of attrition in a society where parental authority is strong.

5. *Failure to be baptized.* Non-Christian Chinese tend to think of baptism in pagan, ritualistic terms and to regard it as the point

of no return. Hence Chinese parents will often grudgingly allow young people to practice their Christian faith but are violently opposed to their being baptized. But in the church and para-church organizations, baptism is seldom given any sacramental significance and so converts see it as rather inconsequential and often do not get baptized. When pressures and temptations come, they can quickly revert to traditional ways and tell themselves that they are not, after all, irreversibly committed to Christianity. Also, having compromised and failed to obey in the area of baptism, other compromises come more easily.

6. *The unequal yoke.* Single girls, through loneliness and intense family pressure, frequently become attached to a non-Christian partner and become inactive.

7. *Nomadic churches.* Lacking facilities of their own, many churches experience a very migratory existence, constantly on the move from one rented place to the next. The change of location or meeting time inevitably proves inconvenient for some members who then drop out. The sheer tiresomeness of frequently having to find the way to a new place of worship by public transport is altogether too much for others. It is not uncommon for a church to have to move two or three times a year.

8. *Churches unstructured for growth.* Eddie Gibbs observed that lapsing rates are higher where membership exceeds 175 and there is only one pastor and an inadequate cellular structure. The lapsing is due to inadequate face-to-face contact and a lack of pastoral care (1981:275-279). Many churches in Singapore are in precisely that situation. The one pastor is overworked and often inexperienced. He is frequently not even sure how to go about building a web of small groups, nor does he understand the importance of doing so. The congregational and cellular structures provide for the social and pastoral needs of members and make it almost impossible for them to slip away unnoticed. At the present time, most churches have so many people in proportion to staff that they never know who they have and who they have lost. In responses from, and about, lapsed members, it was not uncommon to find that they had been gone for three years or more and had never been missed.

9. *Inadequate nurture.* Again, related to pastoral care, socio-

logist of religion John Clammer found that the biggest complaint among Christians was that of a lack of follow up and general nurture (1981:20-25). This lack of shepherding is a problem of structuring and training. Most churches lack an adequate small group structure, and where these do exist, they are seldom thriving because the study materials used are tedious or irrelevant.

10. *A different kind of people.* David Hesselgrave comments that people will revert much more quickly and easily if the church they attend is not made up of their kind of people (1980:277). This sense of fitting and belonging is essential and is one of the reasons why there are few lasting conversions among working class people. There are few churches where they feel at home.

11. *Loneliness.* In an urban society like Singapore, there are many lonely people who come into the church. Many pass out again unwelcomed and unwarmed. All too often reversion is a result of converts experiencing anomie in the church. Anomie is a lostness and confusion that comes when one is in a strange place and fails to feel a part of the situation or to find meaning in it. The church needs to work hard in the area of incorporating newcomers. Most times newcomers are left to try and wriggle their own way into the group, and not uncommonly the "old timers" in their cliques unconsciously close ranks on them.

12. *Felt needs unmet.* People in urban society have a variety of motives for coming to church, and whether those motives and felt needs are legitimate or not, they must be met or there will be a feeling of letdown and disillusionment. This is why it is so important for newcomers to be followed up on an individual basis and in a meaningful manner. A superficial welcome from the pulpit, a handshake at the door, or a visitor's label on the lapel is quite inadequate.

13. *Christianity a crutch.* Christianity in Singapore is proving, for many young people, to be a bridge from the old culture to the new. But it can, in some cases, become a crutch in what is primarily a cultural, socioeconomic problem. Christian workers should be aware of this for, if people become "Christian" without becoming Christians, when they have successfully found their feet in the new world the bridge may be scrapped and they will flow into the secularizing stream of modernity. If their Christianity

is going to stick it must be a true conversion, a genuine spiritual encounter with God.

14. *Social failure of the church.* Finally, the church and parachurch, in their evangelistic effort, have concentrated heavily on the spiritual dimension of conversion, frequently neglecting the cultural and social aspect. As a result, Christianity is often like a partially vulcanized patch on a car tube. It could come off at any time because it has not been melted down into the fabric of the whole man with his social, psychological and economic needs. With Singapore's strongly pietistic expression of Christianity, social activities have often been frowned upon as a waste of energy and resources because they are not "spiritual". But that view must change, for spiritually-changed people also need social fulfilment, and if they fail to find it among Christians, they will find it in their old non-Christian social context.

What can be done to overcome this complex and serious problem of fall-away?

## Overcoming Attrition

I would like to offer eight suggestions.

Churches should begin by giving themselves a little shock treatment. They should calculate and study their membership and adherent turnover levels and face up realistically to the actual dimension of the problem.

Second, there is wide consensus among church diagnosticians that the churches should be prepared to shoulder much of the blame themselves. When a person reverts, the immediate reaction tends to be, "they have backslidden," assuming that all the backward movement has been on the side of the individual. "Their faith was not real," we say, or, "they were insincere or not committed enough." But Schaller warns that we must begin by assuming the integrity of the individual who joins the church. He or she came with a need, expecting the church experience to be fulfilling and helpful, and expecting to stay on. The departure of such a person indicates that the church has probably let them down in some way (1978:115-123). Hesselgrave insists that incorporation is largely the responsibility of the church (1980:282). Often reversions and transfers out are a sign of some spiritual, organizational or quality lack in the life of the church, and a failure to minister to the needs of the whole person.

Third, the quality, attractiveness and usefulness of church programmes must be upgraded. Structures for celebration, congregation and cell must be provided. By listening to tapes of other services, by visiting successful churches, by personal mentoring and by reading, pastors may be helped to a better level of performance. As long as the sheep are wandering away or being stolen, there is some internal deficiency that requires rectifying.

Fourth, new converts and visitors need intensive care to ensure that they are adequately integrated into the life of the church. The pastor cannot do this. He should be the trainer of lay-shepherds. McGavran reminds us that, of those followed up immediately, 90 per cent join the church, 50 per cent of those contacted a week later join, but only 10 per cent of those not contacted for a month will become members (1980:259). There must be such a system of accountability that undershepherds are ashamed to procrastinate. Schaller notes that men are the hardest to assimilate and so will need special attention (1983: 87-88). In Singapore, where newcomers are almost entirely young people, they could be formed into care groups which would be a homogeneous unit. In large churches, one does not need to know everyone, and there is little hope of getting young converts and newcomers into the long-established social units of the church. As long as they have a group to which they belong and in which they are adequately nurtured, they will stay. Welcome dinners and personally matching newcomers with members can also be helpful sometimes, but the social life blood of the church flows best through home groups. These must be created, and great care must be taken in training leaders and providing interesting study materials so that the groups are dynamic and powerful.

Fifth, it is impossible for people to drop out of small groups unnoticed. The other members of a well functioning group are immediately accountable for anyone who ceases to come. But, whatever method the church uses, absentees should be quickly pinpointed and followed up by use of some pastoral care network.

Sixth, members, especially males, must be kept active and involved. We observed in an earlier chapter that males are less likely to feel fulfilled if they have nothing to do. In the study of lapsed members, it was found that quite a number had changed churches in search of some ministry in which to be involved, looking for somewhere where they were needed. They felt the need of a ministry and many no doubt felt the need of the acceptance which an appointment to a church ministry provides. One of the secrets of the Southern Baptist growth is the way they activate their people in service. In one Pentecostal church in Singapore, the pastor is quick to get a care group operating in the home of a newcomer, even to the point of moving one from another home. Participators will not easily drop out.

Seventh, in the case of well educated, high-powered people, the leader's task is not to do everything for them, but to develop the structures in which they can operate.

Finally, Lyle Schaller warns that trying to reactivate lapsed members is a high investment programme, full of frustration and failure. If members become active again, it will be in another church. Many bear resentment against their former church, and in any case, in a shame oriented society, it is very difficult for a person to return after having lapsed.

One of the causes of attrition is the lack of Christian males to partner all the female Christians. This acute problem merits special attention.

## Sexual Imbalance

Within the overall national population today, there are fractionally more males than females. Chinese Religion has slightly more female adherents than males. Hinduism and Islam have a preponderance of males, partly because of the greater number of male immigrants and partly because Indians and Pakistanis tended to send their daughters home to be married. Christianity is a religion of adoption and it is very evident that more females than males have been choosing Christianity. The Census shows that in Protestantism there is a considerable excess of females over males; 55 per cent to 45 per cent. Because more male

Christians are inactive than females, the ratio in the churches is even worse; commonly it is 3 to 1 or 2 to 1. Few churches have a balance of sexes. Catholics do not face the same problem because their growth is mostly biological.

This imbalance in Protestantism is a serious problem for two reasons. First, the church's failure to attract and hold males must cause us to re-examine the presentation of our gospel and the style of our church life. Second, in a society where singleness is not yet acceptable, many single girls are pressured into marrying non-Christians, at which point most become inactive or turn to another religion. Many are being won only to be lost again, not because they failed to love the Lord, but because their rightful and natural need for a life partner could not be fulfilled in the church. Something urgently needs to be done about this state of affairs. To this end I have tried to pinpoint some of the causes and then to contribute some tentative suggestions toward a solution.

## Causes of Imbalance

In my *Twelve Churches Study*, I made a special effort to discover the reasons for this imbalance, and most of the following statistics and conclusions are based on that research.

In chapter 3 we found that women have traditionally been more actively involved in Chinese Religion, while men are more passive in their religious commitment. Thus, when the credibility of the religion is called into question, as it has been by the modernizing world view, womenfolk feel a need for a functional substitute more than do men. And so we found that women were embracing Christianity in larger numbers, while men tended to drift from passive adherence to traditional religion, to passive agnosticism.

There are eight observations that I wish to make based on my research.

First, females are more free to convert. While females are more active in religion, they are less significant. The male is the head of the family, and the care of the ancestors is his ultimate responsibility, as is the continuance of the family line and the preservation of the family honour. When a male wishes to convert, especially the eldest son, there is a lot more family resistance than in the case of a female conversion.,

Second, males are generally more career oriented, and many male converts become absorbed with secular ambition and lapse from active Christian involvement before the age of marriage, thus accentuating the imbalance.

Third, while males tend to be ambitious, aggressive and less dependent on religion, many females are the reverse. They feel much more need for the security and sense of belonging which may be found both in religion and marriage. This appears to be a universal characteristic. William Reyburn, for instance, observed it to be so in French Cameroon (1967:165).

Fourth, in the Chinese cultural context, males are regarded as of superior status and this has its influences. Many fellows take non-Christian girl friends and persuade them to come to church, where they are converted. When a Christian girl takes a non-Christian boy friend, however, she is less often successful in persuading him to follow her way.

Fifth, the sex status phenomenon also makes an impact in the area of witnessing both among friends and in the home. Females are often influenced to convert by males, but males are markedly less often influenced to convert by a female, whether sibling or friend. Thus females are winning mostly females to Christ and males are winning both sexes. The net result of this is more female converts than males.

Sixth, 23 per cent of males came from Christian homes, but only 19 per cent of females did. This means that over the issue of marriage, females are under a good deal more pressure to marry non-Christians.

Seventh, when males did become Christians, they found more fulfilment and spiritual benefit in activity centred aspects of church life where they could do something. Females, on the other hand, were more content with passive roles such as sitting in on a worship service or Bible study. But, unfortunately, most of our churches are not well enough organized to mobilize the laity and so there are very few serving and leading roles open to the fellows. Thus many become disillusioned and often cease to attend. This is especially so in bigger churches.

Finally, males are more aggressive and active in witness. Theirs is a more task oriented approach, such as confronting a person in the street. Females, on the other hand, tend to take a more relational approach, witnessing to friends. The latter method is usually more fruitful than the former but produces almost entirely female converts.

Many of our churches are less than 40 per cent male. For them particularly, this imbalance is an acute problem whether they recognise it or not. And, city wide, it appears to be growing worse not better. What possible solutions are there?

## Corrective Actions

I do not profess to have any final solutions, but there are several things that could help.

In the first place, the quality of preaching and worship must be upgraded if males are to be attracted. While females tend to be attracted to a church primarily because of emotive factors such as friendship and inspiring worship, males are attracted more at the cognitive level. Good preaching, teaching and youth programmes gained their greatest approval ratings in the survey.

Allen Swanson found the same to be true among Chinese in Taiwan, especially among mature men (such as are in short supply in Singapore churches). He cites the offer of an extended Bible study course used by the China Home Bible League as an evangelistic medium. Though the church has a majority of females, this course is attracting a majority of males, and males more than females stay through to the higher level studies, which indicates that they are looking for a challenge. In all, 39 per cent of those taking the course were aged between 31 and 50, and 21 per cent between the ages of 21 and 30 (1978:97-99).

This is an indication that churches desiring to attract men should find ways to place challenges before them. For reasons mentioned earlier in relation to interchurch Crusades, any programme of Bible study or theological education would be better operated at a congregational level than by parachurch organizations, even if the materials were produced by an outside agency such as the China Home Bible League.

Second, in order to attain a more even balance of sexes,

special emphasis is needed on male oriented ministries, such as Boys' Brigades, Boy's Camps and Men's Growth Seminars. The best church leadership should be directed into such ministries. By accident of history, Prinsep Street Presbyterian Church developed a very strong Boys' Brigade movement which is evangelistic as well as social, and over the years this has produced a considerably healthier ratio of sexes in that church.

Mt Carmel Bible Presbyterian has a perfect balance of sexes, the best record I found in any church. There appear to be two secrets for this success. It was established in a low income housing area and has, since its beginning, offered tuition classes to children in the neighbourhood. Because Chinese families generally place more emphasis on male attainment, this programme has contacted many males who have subsequently been converted. Secondly, the pastor has been very forthright in his teaching about not being unequally yoked. But coupled with this, and his refusal to marry any church person to an unbeliever, he has conducted special counselling classes for young couples with non-Christian partners. With love and care, he has graciously given premarital counselling and at the same time shared the gospel and impressed upon them the importance of being in agreement. As a result of this ministry he has seen many girls bring their non-Christian fellows to church, witnessed their conversions, and linked them in Christian marriage.

A third corrective would be for the churches to work at creating structures where their members, especially the males, could find some sort of challenging ministry. Task oriented groups will be especially attractive to men.

Fourth, special effort must be made by church members to help any visiting males to assimilate, because they find social interaction and assimilation more difficult than do females.

Further, the pastor must strenuously avoid a diet of sermons that are introspective and related to domestic issues more than to the business world and to the problems of men. Unfortunately, many pastors are more in touch with domestic affairs, from their own home life and visitation, than they are with the world of men. They therefore need to make a special effort to keep intelligently informed about issues that touch the lives of men.

Finally, the pastor must make a special evangelistic thrust among men, using his own male members to organize business-men's breakfasts and the like.

There remains one more of the church's thorny problems to be discussed in this chapter, and that is the area of community or *koinonia* in the church.

## Poor Community in the Life of the Church

For too long, says Robert Schuller, the church has operated on a wrong definition of herself. Calvin's definition of the church was "*a place* where the Word is proclaimed, sacraments administered, and discipline maintained." Says Schuller,

> The definition ignores emphasizing the most important aspect of the church — which is *a group* of joyful Christians happily sharing their glorious faith with the despairing souls of their fellowmen who have never known the joy of Christ! .... The church is a *corporate group* of happy, Holy Spirit-inspired Christians (1974: 60; emphasis added).

Too often the church has operated on Calvin's definition and lacked the personal touch and warmth of corporality. Too often it has forgotten that the biblical concept of church is a body, a family, an organism. Throughout this study we have repeatedly referred to the need for community in Singapore society, and to the church's chronic failure to demonstrate true community. We return to this subject now because the lack of community is a significant cause of attrition and because it is essential for stable church growth.

To quote Peter Wagner,

> One of the major reasons why people stay in a church once they have joined it is that they find there a quality of love and fellowship that can be found nowhere else. Christian fellowship is highly important in church growth (1981b:282).

Conversely, says Wagner, many churches have bad news to share, not good news. Though they have aggressive evangelistic programmes and baptize many converts, they still fail to grow because they don't really want strangers in their group. And those who are frozen out don't even bother to say good-bye (Wagner 1981b:282).

## The Urban Answer to an Urban Need

In fast changing urban Singapore, social networks have been disrupted through the relocation of the populace and the enormous change in occupational structures. Many are lost, lonely, confused, frustrated and even frightened. The meaning of life evades them and even communication on a family level has broken down. There are deep unmet psychological needs for security, belonging, acceptance and approval.

The church in *koinonia* is the true answer to the urban need. It is the new community, the beginning of God's working out of the reconciliation of all things in Christ, and the agent of that reconciliation in the world. The church is Christ revealing Himself through relationship (Eph. 3:10), but she must start again to be what she is.

The leaders of the church must help her to readjust her ways so that she can live out her true definition as *a people*. For, up to this time, one of the chief criticisms of the church is that she is an "unfriendly" place, full of hypocritical, unfriendly people. Responses on forms returned from lapsed members were mostly of one type: "felt uneasy in the church"; "no encouragement from fellow members"; "too many unfriendly elders ... so that sometimes the thought of going to church makes you sick"; "failed to find real friendship in the church"; "church is too self-centred" and "fellowship is superficial".

I have *six suggestions* to offer which might help the church in Singapore live out her communal role.

As evangelicals, we have been too prone to think of our mission only in terms of evangelism and individual conversions. Converts have too often been heads counted or scalps captured, rather than people loved and integrated into the body. We must learn to think of the whole man with his spiritual, social and psychological needs. If our community life were better, we would not have to threaten people with hell or beat them over the head with words to get a commitment. They would be irresistibly attracted to the church.

Second, churches must provide structures for belonging and help people into them. Small churches grow fast because people are noticed and can be easily known there. The particular type of structure is unimportant so long as it provides a sense of belonging. A small group Bible class can do this, so can a church choir, a coffee club, a missionary committee, a fund raising group and a board of elders. But generally, as has been repeatedly demonstrated through the centuries of church history, the small home meeting, cell or kinship circle has proved to be the most successful dynamic for community.

For a pastor already overburdened with the care of his people, the thought of having to take time to decentralize the church programme into smaller groups, to train group leaders and prepare materials may be overwhelming. But experience has shown that, once these groups are functioning, the calls on the pastor for pastoral care will diminish markedly. He can start to be an overseer, for the groups will do most of the shepherding for him.

Third, great care must be taken not to disrupt what community already exists. The level of community is so low in most churches that one can ill afford to disrupt circles of belonging that are already in operation. The short term Bible school approach is gaining popularity in Singapore. Churches are disbanding their regular Bible classes in favour of centralized, large classes where people enroll for courses on a ten week basis. Teachers are commonly imported for these courses. The standard of informational input is usually better, but the social dimension of the old Bible class is lost. No longer is there the same opportunity for discussion and questions; the student composition of the classes alters every ten weeks, and even the teacher is not known well enough to be easily approachable. This concept, which began in the United States, is being rejected there because of its socially detrimental effect.

Fourth, a number of parachurch organizations have many leaders experienced in the small group dynamic. They could well help in this area by offering training to the churches. And this offer of co-operation could help to reduce the feelings of competition that currently exist.

A fifth point is that the Chinese are activists, more interested in doing than in talking, meditation and subjective self-examination. While self-exposure is one of the keys to fellowship, churches should not institute the tactics of full blown American group therapy too suddenly. Sharing should be developed by stages, and groups will thrive best if they have activities where members can do things together and face challenges and targets.

The next area is one in which the charismatics have a lot to teach other churches. Traditional Chinese society is very reserved. There is a lack of intimacy, and expressions of affection and gratitude do not come easily. If the church is to become the place of warmth, care and encouragement that young Singaporeans want it to be, then there must be a learning of the art of communicating affection and encouragement. This must be done very gradually. Step one is to get people participating in the service, responding verbally to what the pastor says. He can develop the custom of calling for their responses and showing he really expects to have them. Praying for each other in small groups in the service, occasionally clapping or holding hands during singing to express joy and togetherness — all these help to break down the spectator, nonrespondent, passive state of the worshipper. Gradually, through formulae given by the pastor, people can be helped to express words of care, concern and love to others seated nearby, until, by his encouragement and example of outgoing warmth, people are able to start being free to love one another overtly and without embarrassment.

Finally, some of the most warmhearted extrovert members of the church should be assigned the duty of welcoming newcomers. The best people should be on door duty at services. Newcomers need to be enfolded into the church community; they should not have to elbow their way in.

The problems of the church are by no means insurmountable. The three we have dealt with in this chapter are among the most deep-rooted problems the church faces but, as we have seen, there are plenty of corrective actions that might be taken and none of them are so difficult as to be beyond the church's capacity. We now leave specific congregational dilemmas in order to take a more sweeping view of the whole church, endeavouring to discern the path she should take in the years immediately ahead. We will deal particularly with the matter of increasing the harvest through stepping up extension and bridging growth.

## For discussion

1. Prevention is better than cure when tackling the problem of dropouts. Try to assess the reasons why people leave your church. What can be done to arrest this drift?
2. In what ways could your church strengthen its ministry to men?
3. What practical steps might be taken to improve the quality of community in your church? Who could be mobilized to implement these changes?

# Chapter 12
# Planning for Further Growth

The church can grow in four ways: *Internal growth* — the conversion and increased commitment of those already within the church; *Expansion growth* — the increase in size of existing congregations; *Extension growth* — congregations planting daughter churches among their own kind of people and in their own region; *Bridging growth* — congregations and denominations moving out to plant churches among other types of people (McGavran 1980:100).

So far in our study, attention has been focused on internal and expansion growth. But church growth experts unanimously agree that multiplying new units is the fastest means to church growth.

## Multiplying Churches

Small and new churches grow faster than older and larger churches. Young, small churches are usually more eager to grow and more diligent in evangelism. Larger churches tend to carry more passengers unless they are extremely well organized at the small group level. Most people prefer to give birth to something new rather than to maintain an old institution. New units are more vigorous, flexible and free to organize themselves to meet current needs, rather than to follow old traditions. The growth of old churches is usually predominantly biological and by transfer. New churches have more conversion growth and thus an increased contact with the non-Christian community. New churches are necessary for reaching groups of people of different homogeneous units. In fact, because the largest section of the unevangelized world will only be reached by cross-cultural evangelism, the world can never be evangelized without a vast multiplication of new churches.

In this chapter, we will describe the urgent need for a rapid multiplication of churches in Singapore. Attention will be called to the contextual parameters within which this growth must occur; and some preliminary suggestions will be made as to strategy and suitable types of church planting. We begin with the need for multiplication.

## The Current Crisis

A superficial glance at some government statistics would seem to indicate that further multiplication of Christian congregations is wholly unnecessary and unjustifiable. In 1968, a government release showed that Christians already had a disproportionately high number of religious buildings.

| Religion | No. of adherents in 1970 | No. of Sites/Buildings |
|----------|--------------------------|------------------------|
| "Buddhist" | 1,000,000 | 75 |
| Muslim | 283,000 | 83 |
| Hindu | 119,550 | 31 |
| Christian | 92,508 | 81 |
| Sikh | 13,500 | 4 |
| Judaism | 600 | 2 |

(Nyce 1970:42)

**Figure 9**

It is true that Christianity has proportionally far more religious meeting places than any other religion but there are other factors that should be borne in mind before passing judgment on this situation. Buddhism and Christianity, and to a lesser degree, Hinduism and Islam, have religious centres in all sorts of places that are not classified as religious sites. It is estimated that there are over 1,000 centres of Chinese Religion in Singapore, most of these being in the private homes of mediums and independent priests. Christians, of course, also use house churches and meet in an assortment of rented premises.

Further, the purpose and function of the meeting place varies between religions. Centres of Chinese Religion are not meant for congregational worship. Worshippers come individually as and when they need to perform some religious rite. But Christianity is a religion of community; worshippers congregate, and so more accommodation is necessary. Christians also frequent religious sites much more often than do adherents of Chinese Religion who practice most of their religion in the home and only go to a temple or shrine in a crisis or on special occasions. The church actually faces an acute accommodation crisis both at the level of official and unofficial religious sites, a situation that is going to radically slow the reaping of the harvest unless it is remedied.

***Sociological Strangulation.*** The Katong Presbyterian Church grew from chapel services held in the Katong Presbyterian schools. Such was the responsiveness to the gospel experienced that Sunday services were convened in one of the schools for converts from the chapels. Lim Kim-Toin, who has worked in that situation since 1973, describes how he saw 500 per cent growth in six years. A church was built and, during those few years, was expanded three times to cope with a membership that grew to 400. But further extensions on the existing property are now impossible; there is parking for only 20 cars and the surrounding streets are too narrow to permit parking. The Sunday school meets in the girls' school across the street. Seven Bible classes meet in the church and manse on Sunday. Part of the manse has been converted into a much needed nursery so leaving even less room for other classes. Today the growth of that burgeoning church has plateaued because of this lack of physical facilities (Lim 1981:29-43, 56). Wagner describes such a lack of facilities as "sociological strangulation". It is one of his catalogue of church diseases which chokes growth (1979a:88-100).

The story of Katong Presbyterian Church could be repeated any number of times all over Singapore. In fact, this is one of the more fortunate churches in that it has its own facilities, facilities which are, moreover, officially recognized by the government zoning authorities as a church.

Many congregations meet illegally in homes, others rent hotel conference rooms, night clubs, public auditoriums, school class-rooms and so on. It is almost impossible to find any meeting place to rent in the city on Sundays as the Christians have already taken up everything available. Services have been held in such unlikely places as pharmacies, doctors' waiting rooms, in cake shops, out of doors in hawkers' centres, almost anywhere you like to think of. Many of the places are not at all conducive to worship and most hotels and rented places forbid any children's ministry. Not uncommonly, baptismal services are conducted in the sea, or in baths in private homes. The frustrations and inconveniences are considerable, and many people become weary with the struggle to survive in such unsuitable settings.

Rented facilities are mostly of insecure tenure, and what does a church of 400 do, for instance, when on short notice it is informed that its meeting place is to be taken over for the next two Sundays for political rallies, or that some other church has pulled strings with the owner and taken over its tenure of the meeting place? Grace Baptist Church owned a shophouse, and though it was small, hot and inconvenient, it was a legal church meeting place and the crowd could overflow into the market square outside. But then, in 1978, the government bulldozed the building for urban renewal and no replacement accommodation was offered. For four years, the church wandered from place to place all over the city. When the facility obtained was near to convenient transport, comfortable and large enough, the church grew; when it was too small or otherwise uncongenial, members drifted away. For a while the church met in the beautiful facilities of the American School and within a few months, numbers rose from around 300 to 600. But then, when evicted and forced to use a facility beside a noisy, dusty building site in the heat of the tropical afternoon, numbers fell to around 280. In 1982, after 23 years of existence, Grace Baptist finally got its first full time pastor and was able to build its own church for the astronomical sum of U.S.$1.4 million. Within three months, numbers leapt to 600, almost filling the new sanctuary to its capacity of 700. By 1984 it was accommodating 1,000 people every Sunday in multiple services.

With such accommodation problems, a church can quickly fill its building no matter what the size, unless the standard of ministry is pitifully poor. In Singapore, therefore, we are talking about nationwide acute and chronic sociological strangulation.

Some church growth authors stress the value of churches having to struggle to survive and to obtain facilities in their early years. Elmer Towns takes this line, suggesting that the most virile churches are born in adversity (1982:5). Adversity and struggle can, no doubt, be a blessing, but, generally speaking, I believe that Donald McGavran has more of a feel for the Singapore-type situation when he lists as one of the keys to church growth, "surmount the property barrier".

> Congregations must have a place to meet, and house churches furnish an excellent pattern to begin with. But house churches ... under very crowded conditions have great handicaps.
>
> One longs to discover a way in which the enormously wealthy world church can help multiply congregations in Africasian cities, eliminate the bottleneck of high-priced land, and get suitable meeting houses (1980:328).

But even he fails to appreciate the Singapore dilemma, for he goes on to say that the best way to overcome the problem is by making more converts so that they can pay for a building.

Lyle Schaller speaks of the commonly suggested advantages of renting rather than buying: no capital investment, low operating costs, flexibility, intimacy, freedom to move to new, appropriate locations. But he suggests that, while the idea has "romantic appeal", most congregations which try that method decide that the disadvantages outweigh the advantages. Rented premises can usually only cater for small groups, the community sees it as a cheap and shoddy way of doing things, there is poor visibility, the church becomes preoccupied with finding places in which to meet, membership is usually unstable, youth ministry and other activities are curtailed, the setting is often not conducive to worship, there is inadequate storage space, and the method ignores the need of people to feel the security of having their own place (1983:151-152). Singaporean Christians would readily identify with that evaluation, for such problems are even more intense in Singapore than they are in most places in the United States about which Schaller writes. Singapore also faces a further problem that makes church planting and facility development essential.

**Christian Isolation.** In chapter 7 we observed that Christians are heavily middle and upper middle class. Few of the working class have been reached for Christ. The Christians live predominantly in the affluent private sector housing areas, or in the higher income HDB flats. They are geographically, occupationally and socially separated from the largely unevangelized sector of the community.

Further, most of the churches are in the private housing areas, the now largely unpopulated commercial zone, or in rented premises in the hotel and business districts. In 1973, only 27 of Singapore's 187 churches were in or in the vicinity of public housing estates (Wong 1973:128). If anything, the situation has probably worsened since then, and today 75 per cent of the population is located in public housing estates. If the church is to reach the unreached people and adequately serve the reached, the location of churches must adjust to their new living patterns. Fortunately, the public transport system is excellent and can partly compensate for the failure of the church to move with the people.

**Reaching the Neglected Peoples.** There are dialect speakers, mostly older people. There are Indians of various cultures and religious perspectives, and also Muslim Malays who need reaching. This is a cross-cultural evangelism problem. These people, even the few who can speak English, will never be at home in most of the existing congregations. Some people suggest that the two or three remaining Baba congregations could evangelize and church the Malays. This is simply not feasible. It is the young Malays who are most receptive. The Baba churches are old and dying and their people old. And, while their language is called Malay, it is a distinct dialect and the Baba people are Chinese, never were Muslims and have a unique culture and dress which is very different from that of the Malays. Such a strategy is doomed to failure.

Then there is the bulk of the population, classified as working class, who are almost entirely unreached and who will never settle into a church of professionals. Large numbers of new churches are needed for these people. This is over and above the need for more churches to evangelize, out to its fringes, the homogeneous unit of receptive, professional, English-educated Chinese.

Changes must come but there are some contextual "givens" which are powerful determinants in our choice of solutions.

## Parameters Within Which We Must Work

We are beginning to see from this study that there is a unique set of limitations which the culture places upon the church. I wish to list just five of these parameters that are facts of life with which the church planter and strategist must live.

First, when a new housing estate is built (usually accommodating some 250,000 people), one piece of land is allocated for a Christian church. This is sold by tender to the highest bidder. Catholics and a number of Protestant groups compete for the single lot, thus pushing up the price.

Second, in the early 1960's the government had a successful campaign to stamp out Communism. One of the controls brought in was a ban on house meetings. While its primary aim was the elimination of Communist cells, one side effect was to make house churches and regular house meetings illegal. Currently, the government largely turns a blind eye on the widespread use of homes by Christian groups. However, local government officials frequently enforce this law, especially if a neighbour should lodge a complaint about the noise of Christian singing or traffic congestion.

The overall result of this is that many Christian groups feel morally bound not to use homes for Christian meetings. Others do so, but deal with the situation by such expediencies as curtailing singing, blacking out windows, airconditioning the home, and meeting semi-secretly. This means that the house church has little visibility and does not present an inviting look to neighbours who know the faceless building to be a church. The public multi-storey housing blocks are much more strictly controlled than are private housing estates, and as a result, most house churches are to be found in the ever shrinking private sector.

Third, before Independence in 1965, zoning controls were more lax. Many shop houses were used as churches. Residential and industrial land could easily be rezoned for church use. But now, zoning control is stricter. Shops may no longer be used as churches, and the few remaining shop front churches are having difficulty keeping their permit to meet. It is also increasingly difficult to get land rezoned for religious purposes.

I should make it clear that the government is not in any way anti-Christian. On the contrary, it is coming increasingly to see the role of religion in preserving an "acceptable" morality. The root of the problem is shortage of land. Land is the only natural resource of this tiny country, and it has little enough of that. National survival depends on a viable economy, and the government has developed an aggressive programme for national prosperity which very naturally requires a careful stewardship of land. It has set the standard by building multi-storey, high density housing. It also controls industrial development with special emphasis on land intensive industries. In all of this it is little wonder that the church has also been pressured in its use of land, especially as churches are visibly poor stewards of land. They add nothing to the Gross National Product and generally glaringly underutilize their facilities, especially during the week.

Fourth, because house meetings are illegal, rentable facilities inadequate in number and land and building costs too high for prolific multiplication of physical facilities, most churches in Singapore face sociological strangulation. This is true whether the facilities are large or small. Accommodation for the church nationwide is hopelessly inadequate and the crisis is going to become more acute as time passes unless some solution is found.

Fifth, the government has aggressively advertised Singapore as both a tourist centre and an ideal site for international conferences. As a result, the city has an abundance of hotels with conference rooms and also many specially constructed conference centres, On Sundays, these facilities are usually available for hire by churches, but already such meeting places are fully booked by churches, and yet there are still many Christian groups searching for places to meet.

Finally, I want to make some suggestions as to the way ahead for the church in Singapore. The church currently faces two challenges which work against each other. There is the crisis of accommodation which stands in the way of growth, and there is the exceptional receptivity to the gospel in the city at the moment. Matched with that receptivity is a Christian community which is evangelical and full of evangelistic zeal. My first five suggestions relate to the problem of accommodation, while those that follow deal more with the church planting approaches most suitable in the Singapore situation.

## The Way Ahead

### Weekday Congregations
Across the two mile long causeway in Muslim Malaysia, Friday, not Sunday, is the weekly public holiday. Many churches have adapted to this by holding their major services on Friday. With our increasing accommodation crisis, it would seem to me that some churches should consider following this example and having additional worship units which meet on weekday evenings. This approach could well accommodate the many people who have weekend jobs and are on shift work, as well as others who, in order to be with friends, would opt to belong to a weekday congregation.

### Regulation Changes
Perhaps the time has come for the many Christians among the elite of Singapore to use their influence to bring about change

in some government regulations which negatively affect church growth. Christian professional associations, such as the Christian Lawyers' Fellowship, might well lobby for more freedom for house churches, and the making available of more land for religious use in the new towns. Since 1981 the government has been concerned about falling moral standards in the city and is beginning to recognize religion as the major bulwark against moral collapse. As a result, religion is taking a higher priority than previously on the government agenda, so the time may be right for such an approach.

## Denominational Distinctives

Diversity as such is not a bad thing, but it would appear that in the present situation, where only one Christian building may be erected in each new town, denominational barriers should not be allowed to grow too high. Clearly each denomination cannot be represented in every housing estate, and many people are going to have to be content to worship at whatever type of church is accessible to them near their area of domicile. Fortunately, all local trained pastors are coming out of multi-denominational schools and so tend to be weak on traditional Western denominational distinctives. Differences are more noticeable in styles of ministry than in tenets of doctrine.

## Combining Resources

It may be that the way to go in tendering for government land is for several churches to pool their resources and to develop a multi-storey, multi-church complex on the one site. One such experiment is in process now. The pooling of resources has enabled these churches to bid successfully for land. Much patience and grace will be needed in sharing facilities, but it may be the only way for some to go.

## Intensive Use of Facilities

Society can rightly be critical of churches for their gross under utilization of expensive facilities. There must be improvement in this area. Once a church has paid for its facilities, it tends to become complacent in its success and does not have a continuing sense of stewardship for the use of the property. There must be an overcoming of the partisan spirit that leads to churches' refusal to share their facilities with younger, less well endowed churches.

Over and above this, churches should plan on their facilities doubling as perhaps a Community Centre, Tuition Centre, Kindergarten, Drug Rehabilitation Unit, Conference Centre or some such purpose that will not only provide a needed service and build rapport with the community, but will make its land-use more credible in the eyes of the government. This will require innovation and sacrifice, but it could increase receptivity and add to the churches' lists of prospects. Architecture will have to be neutral and buildings planned with sensitivity to their wider use. Loyalty to national goals and good citizenship will demand an adventuresome spirit in this area.

## Methods of Church Planting

Suggestions for structures and methods of implementing a church planting programme cannot be fleshed out here, but a brief description should serve to establish the viable alternatives open to those with a vision for extension or bridging growth.

*Independent Plantings.* An individual pioneer can gather a group of friends or contacts to form a fellowship or Bible Study group. In time this can develop into a service in a home, and as the group grows, it can graduate to rented premises and finally to its own property. Due to the legal limitations on house meetings and the expense of purchasing property, this is a difficult road. The many small stunted house churches in Singapore bear sad testimony to the reality of sociological strangulation and to the difficulty of getting fully launched.

Despite all the limitations of house churches, and even their technical illegality, I believe they will perforce continue to be the main way of planting new congregations. They will especially be the essential ingredient to breaking into the public housing estates with the gospel. Many Christian groups will be unable to find any accommodation other than the homes of their members. The divine mandate to evangelize and congregate demands that we take this avenue at least until there can be a relaxing of restrictions and better sources of accommodation.

**Daughter churches.** The established churches have a vital role they can play in church planting. Sng found that churches in Singapore which had planted daughter churches showed a significantly higher growth rate than others (1979:9) Besides the new growth that results, the mother church experiences renewed vitality from the process of giving birth.

a) Planned birthing. Overcrowding has forced many established churches to buy a second property and siphon off some members to start a new work there. This model has the decided advantage of giving the young church a good start; property, leadership, training and encouragement are given. However the younger, more venturesome members tend to move across to the new work, and they frequently soon become frustrated by the control of the elders from the sponsoring church. Being thus indebted, they have to accept the controls, but they resent them none the less. The Chinese tradition is one of autocratic, hierarchical direction by elders. Elders find it hard to let the fledgling church fly free.

I would suggest that a third party be used as a consultant or mediator in forming the partnering relationship. A major part of his task would be to create a vision and a sense of excited anticipation among the board members of the sponsoring church. He should endeavour to inspire them with a sense of the glorious nature of the mission of establishing a strong, healthy lighthouse for Christ in some dark part of the city. The goal should be to so help and build the infant fellowship that it will become a mature unit, no longer needing to cleave to its parent and no longer requiring direction. The rejoicing on the part of the sponsor should result from achieving that goal quickly.

It is far better to establish the purpose and guidelines for the relationship right at the beginning. Emotions always run high if solutions must be sought after the problems have arisen.

b) Adoption. Wagner suggests that established churches adopt struggling, independent new works. This idea should be investigated fully as it has real possibilities for the Singapore situation. Many young churches could be saved from stagnation or failure if assisted with leadership training and the obtaining of property. Here is a missionary opportunity for the more established

churches which are financially stable and own their facilities.
*Splits.* As mentioned earlier, these painful but fruitful plantings are very common in Singapore and will continue to be so.
*Satellites.* a) The Gathered Satellite. This is where all congregations use the one set of facilities and remain under the same
church government. This approach should be one of our central
church planting strategies. It is ideal for developing dialect congregations, new English language congregations for minority groups,
or merely for overcoming crowding in the existing services. Given
the acute shortage of pastors and facilities in Singapore, this
increased use of existing facilities has much to commend it.

b) The Scattered Satellite. Due to the problem of autocratic
control from the mother church, it is probably better to aim
at independence rather than holding the new work as a satellite.

However, Paul Yonggi Cho's Full Gospel Church in Seoul,
Korea is a model that does have real possibilities as a method
for dealing with overcrowding. The large church is divided into
congregations which meet in houses on Sundays and come to
the central church for services on a rotation basis, say once a
month. Thus all members receive adequate nurture and fellowship and also benefit by the central celebration.

*Multi-congregational churches.* These congregations use the same
facilities, but have more autonomy than in the Gathered Satellite
model. This concept could be used for planting dialect congregations by an English language church. But its greatest potential
is for planting much needed congregations of working class people. Help must be given, but every effort made to avoid being
overbearing and paternalistic in the process. The new unit must
not be overshadowed or humiliated by the superior talent of the
sponsoring congregation, nor should it be squashed by many
controls. A church that is financially well off could provide
facilities and guidance by the senior pastor, but let the new
congregation be self-governing. Some very sensitive middle class
people would be needed as cross-cultural missionaries for the
establishing of this type of work.

*Special agency plants.* Denominations need to have well funded
and well staffed departments for the specific purpose of church
planting. Some of the local parachurch evangelistic agencies, such
as the Asia Evangelistic Fellowship (AEF), might also assist in

the development of nationwide church planting programmes which are based on sound demographic studies. The churches are full of zealous, recent converts who have many non-Christian contacts. Many of these are eager to serve, but are often frustrated in the churches because there is nothing for them to do. This energy might easily be utilized in the development of church planting teams. Further, denominations have a stronger financial base from which to tender for the "religious" land in the new towns. If that fails, churches should seek land on the main routes out of the major estates. Accessibility and visibility are crucial.

**Worship units.** This is not strictly a technique for church planting. It is well established that new works grow the fastest. The crisis of facility shortage is patently clear. The concern of the government that facilities be intensively used must be remembered. In light of this, it may be helpful to strategize, not just in terms of the number of new churches planted, but also in terms of the number of new "worship units" started. A "worship unit" refers to actual services held. The addition of these units is a cross between expansion and extension growth.

The most acute problems of the church in Singapore are the happy problems of handling an overwhelming response to the gospel. Our problems are those of growth. Singapore is joining the ranks of the most Christian nations, as Protestantism here and throughout much of Asia (N.E. India, Indonesia, S. Korea, Taiwan and Hong Kong) is growing more rapidly than any other religion in the area. The Lord of the harvest has prepared a bountiful harvest, and we must go forward to reap it, refusing to allow His purposes to be thwarted by obstacles. These can be overcome, but only if we approach them with confidence in the One who can and will remove mountains in response to the faith of His people.

## For discussion

The option for churches is growth or stagnation. What plans is your church making, or could it make, for further growth outward? Are these for expansion, extension or bridging growth? What particular obstacles does the church face and how may these be overcome?

# Conclusion

In all this planning, strategizing and struggling with contextual "givens", it must be remembered that church planting and church growth is ultimately and primarily a spiritual phenomenon. It needs to be stressed that, while the study of sociological, economic and political influences on church growth can make us much more efficient and intelligent workers, the battle is in the spiritual realm. The inner life of the Christians, especially of Christian workers, and the moving of the Holy Spirit are the ultimate keys to growth. Knowledge alone will never result in growing churches. There is no technique nor series of approaches that constitute a royal road to the sort of church growth that is willed by the Holy Spirit. No amount of research into the life and problems of today's communities is going to bring the lost out of darkness into light. Without the exhausting and enlightened labours of sacrificial service and believing prayer, the dying will not be saved. Without the empowering of the Holy Spirit and the spiritual health of the witnesses, there will be no true harvest. We are called into a divine partnering in the building of the Kingdom.

The Spirit is moving in the city of Singapore at this time. He has prepared the context for harvest. He has softened the hearts of a large proportion of the population, so creating a unique receptivity to the gospel of Christ which alone can gloriously redeem lives and transform cities. He sent in an assortment of evangelistic, parachurch organizations just as the harvest began to whiten, ready for the reapers. Today, the sheer numbers of first generation believers, by their zeal and evangelistic fervour, have created a momentum and wave of conversions that could not easily be stopped. Singapore is turning to Christ! The English-educated Chinese community is now a reached people, with over 20 per cent being self-confessed Christians. They need no further outside help in order to evangelize their own homogeneous unit out to its fringes. The working class and dialect speakers too show definite signs of unprecedented receptivity. In the words of Donald McGavran,

> To win the winnable while they are winnable would, indeed, seem to be an urgent priority. The evangelization of the receptive sections of the masses is the best gift we can give to them (1980:294).

Bearing Singapore in mind, let us conclude with a few lines from a city pastor's prayer:

> Give us to know that Thou dost love
> each soul that Thou hast made;
> That size does not diminish grace,
> nor concrete hide Thy gaze.
>
> Grant us, O God, who labor here
> within the throbbing maze,
> A forward-looking, saving hope
> to galvanize our days.
>
> (Ernest Campbell)

# Glossary

*Adherent* — Regular supporter and church attender but not committed to membership.

*Affective* — Attitudes and emotions, as opposed to that which relates to informational and rational thought (cognitive).

*Anomie* — A lostness and confusion that comes when one is in a strange place and fails to feel a part of the situation or to find meaning in it.

*Anthropocentric* — Man centred.

*Anthropology* — The scientific study of mankind, especially of his origins, development, customs and beliefs.

*Attrition* — "Dropouts". The voluntary departure of members from a church.

*Babas* — Descendants of the Chinese settlers from the early Straits Settlements who have adopted a form of Malay culture, dress and language and, in some cases, intermarried with Malays.

*Biological growth* — Children from Christian homes who become members of the church.

*Bridging growth* — Congregations and denominations moving out to plant churches among other types of people: i.e. ethnically, linguistically or socially different from themselves.

*Centrifugal evangelism* — When people go out from the church into the world to witness.

*Centripetal evangelism* — When the life of the church attracts people to itself in such a way that they are converted.

*Chicago School* — The department of the University of Chicago which, in the 1920s, developed urban sociology as a science.

*Conglomerate churches* — Churches that deliberately cater for more than one ethnic, linguistic or class grouping.

*Contextual factors* — Forces operating external to the church and influencing it.

*Continuum* — Something that extends continuously from one point to another: e.g. the line representing the gradual shift in emphasis from one point of view to another.

*Demographic study* — A study of population statistics relating to births, deceases, geographical location, income distribution, education, etc.

*DGR* = Decadal Growth Rate — The growth of a church over a ten year period expressed as a percentage.

*Egocentric* — Self-centred.

*Expansion growth* — The increase in size of existing congregations.

*Extension growth* — Congregations planting daughter churches among their own kind of people.

*HDB* — Housing Development Board.

*Heterogeneity* — Made up of people or things that are unlike each other.

*Homogeneity* — Of the same kind as others, formed of parts that are all of the same kind.

*Homogeneous unit* — Any group of people who perceive themselves to be the same type of people as each other — a social class, ethnic, linguistic or occupational group.

*Homogeneous Unit Principle* — People like to become Christians without having to cross racial, linguistic or class barriers to do so.

*Institutional factors* — The forces of church growth internal to the church herself.

*Intracongregational* — Within a congregation.

*Macro view* — An overall picture.

*Mega-church* — A large church, usually over 2,000 members.

*Micro view* — Viewing the parts from close up.

*Microcosm* — A miniature of something larger.

*Multiplex* — Where the circles of interpersonal relationships, e.g. relatives, workmates, friends, worshippers and neighbours, have a minimum of overlap: i.e. an individual will relate to a largely different set of people in each circle. Multiplex relationships are characteristic of urban life.

*Network* — A chain of interconnected people.

*Nuclear family* — Father, mother and children living as a household.

*PAP* — People's Action Party. The party governing Singapore since it obtained independence from Britain.

*Parachurch* — Christian agencies linked to the church and engaged in a particular aspect of Christian ministry, but existing as independent institutions, separate from congregational and denominational structures.

*Parameters* — Restrictions or boundaries of a particular situation.

*People, A* — A tribe, clan, linguistic or social group; any tightly-knit segment of society.

*People Movement* — Where "a people" converts to Christianity rapidly as a result of multi-individual, mutually-interdependent decisions.

*Prescriptive* — Prescribed by custom and culture.

*Simplex societies* — Where a single group of people relate to each other at every level of life: they are relatives, workmates, friends, worshippers and make up one community. Usually characteristic of rural life.

*Social pathology* — The disorders and ills experienced by a society.

*Socialization* — The process by which the values and social patterns of a people are established.

*Societal* — Of society.

*Sociological strangulation* — When the growth and ministry of a church is inhibited by lack of physical facilities.

*Sociology* — The scientific study of human society and its development and institutions, or of social problems.

*Reached people* — When the church among an ethnic, linguistic or social group of people is strong enough to evangelize the rest of the people in that group without outside help. "A people" is normally regarded as "reached" when 20% of the group is Christian.

*Utilitarianism* — The value system that regards actions as right if they bring useful or desirable results: a form of pragmatism.

*Worldview* — The set of values and beliefs held by an individual or group that sets the patterns for every sector of life: religion, family, economics, social interaction, etc.

# BIBLIOGRAPHY

Addison, James Thayer
 1925    Chinese Ancestor Worship: A Study of its Meaning and its
         Relations with Christianity. The Church Literature Com-
         mittee and SPCK.

Allen, Roland
 1960    The Spontaneous Expansion of the Church. London: World
         Dominion Press.

Balhetchet, Robert P.
 1976    Metamorphosis of a Church, a Study on the People of God in the
         Republic of Singapore: Analysis and Projection. Rome.

Banfield, Edward
 1970    The Unheavenly City. Boston: Little, Brown and Co.

Baptist Mission
 1975    Report of the In-Depth Study Committee of the Malaysia-
         Singapore Baptist Mission.

Baumann, Dan
 1976    All Originality Makes a Dull Church. Santa Ana, California:
         Vision House Publishers.

Benjamin, Geoffrey
 1976    "The Cultural Logic of Singapore's 'Multiracialism'." In
         Singapore: Society in Transition. Riaz Hassan, ed. pp.115-133.
         Kuala Lumpur: Oxford University Press.

Chambers, Calvin H.
 1980    In Spirit and in Truth: Charismatic Worship and the Reformed
         Tradition. Pennsylvania: Dorrance & Co.

Chan, Heng Chee
 1973    Succession and Generational Change in Singapore. Occasional
         Paper No. 3. Department of Political Science, University
         of Singapore.

 1976    "The Political System and Political Change". In Singa-
         pore: Society in Transition. Riaz Hassan, ed.    pp.30-51.
         Kuala Lumpur: Oxford University Press.

Chan, Heng Chee and Hans-Dieter Evers
    1978     "National Identity and Nation Building in Singapore".
             In *Studies in Asean Sociology: Urban Society and Social Change*.
             Peter S.J. Chen and Hans-Dieter Evers, ed.  pp.117-129.
             Singapore: Chopman Enterprises.

Chaney, Charles L.
    1982     *Church Planting at the End of the Twentieth Century*. Wheaton,
             Illinois: Tyndale House Publishers.

Chang, Chen-Tung
    1975     "A Sociological Study of Neighbourliness". In *Public Housing
             in Singapore: A Multi-disciplinary Study*. Stephen H.K. Yeh,
             ed.  pp.281-301. Singapore University Press.

Chen, Peter S.J.
    1976     *Asian Values in a Modernizing Society: A Sociological
             Perspective*. Sociology Working Paper No. 51. Department
             of Sociology, University of Singapore.

    1978a    "Professional and Intellectual Elites in Singapore". In *Studies
             in Asean Sociology: Urban Society and Social Change*. Peter
             S.J. Chen and Hans-Dieter Evers, ed.  pp.27-37. Singapore:
             Chopman Enterprises.

    1978b    "Socio-Psychological Implications of High-Density Living:
             With Special Reference to Singapore". In *Studies in Asean
             Sociology: Urban Society and Social Change*. Peter S.J. Chen
             and Hans-Dieter Evers, ed.  pp. 388-401. Singapore: Chop-
             man Enterprises.

Chen, Peter S. J. and Hans-Dieter Evers, ed.
    1978     *Studies in Asean Sociology: Urban Society and Social Change*.
             Singapore: Chopman Enterprises.

Chen, Peter S.J. and Tai Ching Ling
    1977     *Social Ecology of Singapore*. Singapore: Federal Publications.
    1978     "Urban and Rural Living in a Highly Urbanised Society".
             In *Studies in Asean Sociology: Urban Society and Social Change*.
             Peter S.J. Chen and Hans-Dieter Evers, ed.  pp.406-421.
             Singapore: Chopman Enterprises.

Chiew, Seen-Kong
    1978     "National Integration: The Case of Singapore". In *Studies
             in Asean Sociology: Urban Society and Social Change*. Peter
             S.J. Chen and Hans-Dieter Evers ed.  pp.130-145.

Cho, Paul Yonggi
   1979     *The Fourth Dimension.* New Jersey: Logos International.
Choa, Beng Huat
   1982     "Singapore in 1981: Problems in New Beginnings". In
            *Southeast Asian Affairs* 1982. Huynh Kim Khanh, ed. pp.
            320-335. Singapore: Heinemann Asia.
Choe, Alan F.C.
   1975     "Urban Renewal". In *Public Housing in Singapore: A Multi-
            disciplinary Study.* Stephen H.K. Yeh, ed.   pp. 97-116.
            Singapore University Press.
Clammer, John R.
   1978     "Sociological Analysis of the Overseas Chinese in Southeast
            Asia". In *Studies in Asean Sociology: Urban Society and Social
            Change.* Peter S. J. Chen and Hans-Dieter Evers, ed.
            pp. 170-183. Singapore: Chopman Enterprises.
   1981     *The Social Structure of Religion: A Sociological Study of
            Christianity in Singapore.* Unpublished Paper. Department of
            Sociology, University of Singapore.
Clasper, Paul
   1977     "Christian Spirituality and Chinese Context". In *Ching Feng:
            Quarterly Notes on Christianity and Chinese Religion and
            Culture.* xx, 1, pp. 2-17.
Cooley, Charles Horton
   1966     "The Primary Group". In *Exploring the Ways of Mankind.*
            Walter Goldschmidt ed.   pp. 280-283. New York: Holt,
            Rinehart and Winston.
Cox, Harvey
   1965     *The Secular City.* New York: The Macmillan Company.
Dayton, Edward R. and David A. Fraser
   1980     *Planning Strategies for World Evangelization.* Grand Rapids:
            William B. Eerdmans Publishing Co.
Eames, Edwin and Judith Granich Goode
   1977     *Anthropology of the City.* Englewood Cliffs, New Jersey:
            Prentice-Hall Inc.
Edwards, Betty
   1979     *Drawing on the Right Side of the Brain.* Los Angeles: J.P.
            Tarcher.

Ellul, Jaques
  1970    *The Meaning of the City.* Grand Rapids: Wm. B. Eerdmans
          Publishing Co.

Engstrom, Ted
  1976    *The Making of a Christian Leader.* Grand Rapids: Zondervan
          Publishing House.

Evers, Hans-Dieter
  1978    "The Culture of Malaysian Urbanization: Malay and Chinese
          Conceptions of Space". In *Studies in Asean Sociology: Urban
          Society and Social Change.* Peter S.J. Chen and Hans-Dieter
          Evers, ed.  pp. 333-343. Singapore: Chopman Enterprises.

Finnell, David
  1981    *A Preliminary Report on Research for the Long-Range Plans of
          the Baptist Centre for Urban Studies.* Unpublished Paper,
          Singapore.

Gates, Alen Frederick
  1966    *Church Growth in Taiwan.* D. Miss. Dissertation, Fuller
          Theological Seminary, School of World Mission.

Gibbs, Eddie
  1977    *Urban Church Growth: Clues from South America and Britain.*
          Grove Booklet No. 55. Bramcote, Notts, England: Grove
          Books.

  1981    *I Believe in Church Growth.* Grand Rapids: Wm B. Eerdmans.

Goh, Hwee Huang
  1976    *The Social and Psychological Implications of Relocation: A
          Case Study.* Unpublished paper. Department of Sociology,
          National University of Singapore.

Goh, Yue Yun
  1981    *Religious Activities of University Students: A Study of the
          Campus Crusade for Christ and the Varsity Christian Fellowship.*
          Unpublished paper. Department of Sociology, National
          University of Singapore.

Gopinathan, S.
  1976    "Towards a National Educational System". In *Singapore:
          Society in Transition.* Riaz Hassan, ed.  pp. 67-83. Kuala
          Lumpur: Oxford University Press.

Greenway, Roger S., ed.
  1979    *Discipling the City: Theological Reflections on Urban Mission.*
          Grand Rapids, Michigan: Baker Book House.

Hassan, Riaz

1970    "Population Change and Urbanization in Singapore". In *Analysis of an Asian Society — Singapore*. Riaz Hassan and Joseph B. Tamney, ed. pp. 1-22. University of Singapore.

1971    "The Urban Environment and Mental Health — with Special Reference to Singapore and Other Developing Countries". In *Review of Southeast Asian Studies* Vol: 1:2:48-65. Singapore.

1976    "Public Housing". In *Singapore: Society in Transition*. Riaz Hassan ed. pp. 240-265. Kuala Lumpur: Oxford University Press.

1977    "Social and Psychological Consequences of Household Crowding". In *Southeast Asian Affairs 1977*. Huynh Kim Khanh, ed. pp. 230-236. Singapore: Heinemann Asia.

Hassan, Riaz and Joseph B. Tamney, ed.

1970    *Analysis of an Asian Society — Singapore*. Unpublished papers. Department of Sociology, University of Singapore.

Hesselgrave, David J.

1980    *Planting Churches Cross-Culturally*. Grand Rapids: Baker Book House.

Hinton, Keith W.

1982    *12 Churches Study*. Singapore: Unpublished.

1983    *Toward a Development of Chinese Christian Festivals for the Church in Singapore and Malaysia*. Unpublished paper.

Ho, Wing Meng

1976a    "By Way of An Introduction: Singapore and the Concept of a Global City". In *The Future Singapore — the Global City*. Wee Teong Boo, ed. pp. 108-115. Singapore: University Education Press.

1976b    "The Dialectics of Materialism — Socio-Political Aspects". In *The Future Singapore — The Global City*. Wee Teong Boo, ed. pp. 119-131. Singapore: University Education Press.

Hoge, Dean R. and David A. Roozen, ed.

1979    *Understanding Church Growth and Decline: 1950-1978*. New York: The Pilgrim Press.

Housing Development Board

1982    *HDB Annual Report 81/82*. Singapore: Housing Development Board.

Hsieh, Jiann

　1978　"The Chinese Community in Singapore: The Internal Structure and Its Basic Constituents". In *Studies in Asean Sociology: Urban and Social Change.* Peter S.J. Chen and Hans-Dieter Evers, ed. pp.184-226. Singapore: Chopman Enterprises.

Kane, Herbert

　1976　*Christian Missions in Biblical Perspective.* Grand Rapids: Baker Book House.

Kao, Keng-Kai, Dorothy Kao and Aw Lyn

　1982　*Singapore Church Directory 1982-1983.* Singapore Every Home Crusade Ltd.

Kelley, Dean M.

　1972　*Why Conservative Churches Are Growing: A Study in Sociology of Religion.* New York: Harper and Row Publishers.

Khanh, Huynh Kim, ed.

　1977　*Southeast Asian Affairs 1977.* Singapore: Heinemann Asia.

　1982　*Southeast Asian Affairs 1982.* Singapore: Heinemann Asia.

Khoo, Chian Kim

　1981a　*Census of Population 1980 Singapore. Release No. 7. Income and Transport.* Singapore: Department of Statistics.

　1981b　*Census of Population 1980 Singapore. Release No. 9. Religion and Fertility.* Singapore: Department of Statistics.

Koh, Tai Ann

　1980　"The Singapore Experience: Cultural Development in the Global Village". In *Southeast Asian Affairs 1980.* Leo Suryadinata, ed. pp. 292-307. Singapore: Heinemann Asia.

Koyama, Kosuke

　1974　*Waterbuffalo Theology.* Maryknoll, New York: Orbis Books.

Kraft, Charles H.

　1979　*Christianity in Culture.* Maryknoll, New York: Orbis Books.

Kraft, Marguerite

　1978　*Worldview and the Communication of the Gospel.* Pasadena: William Carey Library.

Kromminga, Carl G.

　1979　"The Role of the Laity in Urban Evangelization". In *Discipling the City.* Roger S. Greenway, ed.　　pp. 128-150. Grand Rapids: Baker Book House.

Kuo, Eddie C.Y. and Aline K. Wong, editors.
1979a    *The Contemporary Family in Singapore: Structure and Change.*
         Singapore: University of Singapore.

Kuo, Eddie C.Y. and Aline K. Wong
1979b    "Some Observations on the Study of Family Change in
         Singapore". In *The Contemporary Family in Singapore: Structure
         and Change.* Eddie C.Y. Kuo and Aline K. Wong ed.  pp.
         3-14. Singapore University Press.

Kwok, Lai Cheng; Lim Pek Hong and John MacDougall
1970     "An Exploratory Study of Aspirations for Self, Com-
         munity and Country among University of Singapore
         Students". In *Analysis of an Asian Society — Singapore.*
         Riaz Hassan and Joseph B. Tamney, ed.  pp. 149-162.
         University of Singapore.

Latourette, Kenneth Scott
1953     *A History of Christianity.* New York: Harper and Row
         Publishers.

Law, Gail M.W.
1981     "Reaching Chinese Factory Workers in Hong Kong". In
         *Unreached Peoples '81.* C. Peter Wagner and Edward R.
         Dayton, ed.  pp.89-102. Illinois: David C. Cook Publishing
         Co.

Lee, Sheng Yi
1978     "Business Elites in Singapore". In *Studies in Asian Sociology:
         Urban Society and Social Change.* Peter S.J. Chen and Hans-
         Dieter Evers, ed.  pp.38-60. Singapore: Chopman Enter-
         prises.

Lee, Soo-Ann
1976     "Human Values and Economic Change in Singapore".
         In *The Future Singapore — the Global City.* Wee Teong
         Boo, ed.  pp. 116-118. Singapore: University Education
         Press.

Leech, Kenneth
1980     *Soul Friend.* San Francisco: Harper and Row, Publishers.

Lefrancois, Guy R.
1972     *Psychology for Teaching.* Belmont, California: Wadsworth
         Publishing Company.

Lim, Joo-Jock
1980     "Bold Internal Decisions, Emphatic External Outlook".

In *Southeast Asian Affairs 1980*. Leo Suryadinata, ed. pp. 270-291. Institute of Southeast Asian Studies. Singapore: Heinemann Asia.

Lim, Kim Toin

1981    A *Practical Design for the Growth and Development of Katong Presbyterian Church in Singapore.* Unpublished D. Min. Dissertation. Fuller Theological Seminary.

Liu, Thai Ker

1975    "Design for Better Living Conditions". In *Public Housing in Singapore: A Multi-disciplinary Study*. Stephen H.K. Yeh, ed. pp.115-184. Singapore University Press.

Luzbetak, Louis J.

1970    *The Church and Cultures*. Pasadena, California: William Carey Library.

Lyall, Leslie

1961    *John Sung*. London: China Inland Mission.

Manis, Jerome G.

1970    "Conceptions of Social Stratification in Singapore: An Exploratory Research". In *Analysis of an Asian Society*. Riaz Hassan and Joseph B. Tamney, ed.  pp.115-125. University of Singapore.

McDonough, Reginald M.

1979    *Keys to Effective Motivation*. Nashville: Broadman Press.

McGavran, Donald A.

1979    *Ethnic Realities and the Church*. Pasadena, California: William Carey Library.

1980    *Understanding Church Growth*. Grand Rapids, Michigan: Wm. B. Eerdmans Publishing Co.

1981    "Why Some American Churches are Growing and Some are Not". In *The Complete Book of Church Growth*. Elmer L. Towns, John N. Vaughan and David J. Seifert, eds.  pp. 284-294. Wheaton, Illinois: Tyndale House Publishers.

Ministry of Culture

1982    *Singapore '81*. Singapore: Ministry of Culture.

Montgomery, James H. and Donald A. McGavran
 1980    *The Discipling of a Nation*. Santa Clara, California: Global
          Church Growth Bulletin.
Nyce, Ray
 1970    *The Kingdom and Country: A Singapore Area Research Project
          Report*. Singapore: Unpublished document presented to
          The Lutheran Church in Malaysia and Singapore and The
          Board of World Missions, LCA.
Palen, J. John
 1981    *The Urban World*. New York: McGraw-Hill Book Company.
Presbyterian Church in Singapore, The
 1977    Minutes of the Third Session of the Synod and Other
          Papers.
Quah, Jon S.T.
 1975    "Singapore's Experience in Public Housing: Some Lessons
          for Other States". In *Political and Social Change in Singapore*.
          Southeast Asian Perspectives No. 3. University of Singapore.
Rajaratnam, S.
 1976    "Singapore: Global City". In *The Future of Singapore — the
          Global City*. Wee Teong Boo, ed.   pp.15-24, Singapore:
          University Education Press.
Redfield, Robert
 1941    *The Folk Culture of Yucatan*. Chicago: University of Chicago
          Press.
Redfield, Robert and Milton Singer
 1954    *The Cultural Role of Cities*. Chicago: University of Chicago
          Press.
Redford, Jack
 1978    *Planting New Churches*. Nashville: Broadman Press.
Reyburn, William D.
 1967    "The Church, Male and Female". In *Readings in Missionary
          Anthropology*. William A. Smalley, ed.  pp.195-198. New
          York: Practical Anthropology.
Roberts, Vella-Kottarathil
 1981    *The Urban Mission of the Church from an Urban Anthropological
          Perspective*. D. Miss. Dissertation. Fuller Theological
          Seminary, School of World Mission.

Roof, Hoge, Dyble et al.

1979 "Factors Producing Growth or Decline in United Presbyterian Congregations". In *Understanding Church Growth and Decline: 1950-1978*. Dean R. Hoge and David A. Roozen, ed. pp. 198-223. New York: The Pilgrim Press.

Roof, Wade Clark, et al.

1979 "Factors Producing Growth or Decline in United Presbyterian Congregations". In *Understanding Church Growth and Decline: 1950-1978*. Dean R. Hoge and David A. Roozen, ed. pp. 198-223. New York: The Pilgrim Press.

Rooy, Sidney H.

1979 "Theological Education for Urban Mission". In *Discipling the City: Theological Reflections on Urban Mission*. Roger S. Greenway, ed. pp. 175-207. Grand Rapids: Baker Book House.

Schaller, Lyle E.

1974 *The Decision-Makers*. Nashville: Abingdon.

1978 *Assimilating New Members*. Nashville: Abingdon.

1983 *Growing Plans: Strategies to Increase Your Church's Membership*: Nashville: Abingdon.

Schuller, Robert H.

1974 *Your Church Has Real Possibilities*. Ventura, California: Regal Books.

Sim, Robert

1980 "Another Set of Statistics: An Analysis of Singapore Graham Crusade". *Impact*, Aug.-Sept. 1980. Singapore: Youth For Christ.

Sng, Bobby E.K.

1979 "Christian Churches in Singapore 1979". *Impetus*. Dec. 1979.

1980a "Christian Profile 1979". In *Impetus*, March 1980.

1980b *In His Good Time: The Story of the Church in Singapore 1819-1978*. Singapore: Graduates' Christian Fellowship.

Sng, Bobby E.K. and You Poh Seng

1982 *Religious Trends in Singapore with Special Reference to Christianity*. Singapore: Graduates' Christian Fellowship and Fellowship of Evangelical Students.

Snyder, Howard A.
   1975    *The Problem of Wineskins: Church Structure in a Technological Age*. Illinois: Inter-Varsity Press.
   1977    *The Community of the King*. Illinois: Inter-Varsity Press.
Spengler, Oswald
   1928    *The Decline of the West II*. New York: Alfred A. Knopf Press.
Suryadinata, Leo, ed.
   1980    *Southeast Asian Affairs 1980*. Singapore: Heinemann Asia.
Swanson, Allen J.
   1971    *Taiwan: Mainline Versus Independent Church Growth*. Pasadena: William Carey Library.
   1981    *The Church in Taiwan: Profile 1980*. Pasadena: William Carey Library.
Swanson, Allen J. ed.
   1978    *I Will Build My Church: Ten Case Studies of Church Growth in Taiwan*. Pasadena: William Carey Library.
Tamney, Joseph B.
   1970a    "An Analysis of the Decline of Allegiance to Chinese Religions: A Comparison of University Students and their Parents". In *Analysis of An Asian Society — Singapore*. Riaz Hassan and Joseph B. Tamney, ed. pp.247-273. University of Singapore.
   1970b    "The Reality of Religious Labels: A Study of Religion Among Singapore University Students". In *Analysis of an Asian Society — Singapore*. Riaz Hassan and Joseph B. Tamney, ed. pp.77-100. University of Singapore.
   1971    "A Sociological Approach to Buddhism in Singapore". *Ching Feng: Quarterly Notes on Christianity and Chinese Religion and Culture*, Vol. XIV:4:153-156.
Teh, Cheang Wan
   1975    "Public Housing in Singapore: An Overview". In *Public Housing in Singapore: A Multi-disciplinary Study*. Stephen H.K. Yeh, ed. pp.1-21. Singapore University Press.
Tham, Seong Chee
   1974    "The Culture Process in Southeast Asia". In *Review of Southeast Asian Studies*, Vol. IV:1-2:11-22.
Thompson, George G.
   1978    "The Political Elite in Singapore". In *Studies in Asian*

               *Sociology: Urban Society and Social Change.* Peter S.J. Chen and Hans-Dieter Evers, ed. pp. 61-73. Singapore: Chopman Enterprises.

Thompson, Lawrence G.

1969      *Chinese Religion: An Introduction.* Belmont, California: Dickerson Publishing Co.

Towns, Elmer L.

1973      *America's Fastest Growing Churches.* Nashville: Impact Books.

1982      *Getting Churches Started.* Privately Published.

Towns, Elmer L., John N. Vaughan and David J. Seifert

1981      *The Complete Book of Church Growth.* Wheaton, Illinois: Tyndale House Publishers.

Wagner, C. Peter

1971      *Frontiers in Missionary Strategy.* Chicago: Moody Press.

1979a     *Your Church Can Be Healthy.* Nashville: Abingdon.

1979b     *Your Spiritual Gifts Can Help Your Church Grow.* Ventura, California: Regal Books.

1981a     *Church Growth and the Whole Gospel.* San Francisco: Harper and Row Publishers.

1981b     "Three Growth Principles for a Soul Winning Church". In *The Complete Book of Church Growth.* Elmer L. Towns, John N. Vaughan and David J. Seifert, ed. pp. 279-283. Wheaton, Illinois: Tyndale House Publishers.

1984a     *Leading Your Church to Growth.* Ventura: Regal Books.

1984b     *Your Church Can Grow: Seven Vital Signs of a Healthy Church.* Ventura: Regal Books.

Walter, Michael A.H.B.

1978      "The Territorial and Social: Perspectives on the Lack of Community in High-Rise/High-Density Living in Singapore". In *Ekistics* 270, June 1978: 236-248. Athens.

Warren, Rachelle B. and Donald I. Warren

1977      *The Neighbourhood Organizer's Handbook.* Notre Dame: The University of Notre Dame Press.

Watson, David

1977      *I Believe in Evangelism.* Grand Rapids: Wm B. Eerdmans Publishing Co.

1978      *I Believe in the Church.* Grand Rapids: Wm B. Eerdmans Publishing Co.

Wee, Teong Boo, ed.
1976    The Future of Singapore — the Global City. Singapore: University Education Press.

Wee, Vivienne
1977    Religion and Ritual Among the Chinese of Singapore: An Ethnographic Study. M.A. Thesis. University of Singapore.

Wirth, Louis
1938    "Urbanism as a Way of Life". American Journal of Sociology, 44:1-24.

Wong, Aline K. and Eddie C.Y. Kuo
1979a   "The Urban Kinship Network in Singapore". In The Contemporary Family in Singapore: Structure and Change. Eddie C.Y. Kuo and Aline K. Wong, ed. pp. 17-39. Singapore University Press.

1979b   "Women's Status and Changing Family Values". In The Contemporary Family in Singapore: Structure and Change. Eddie C.Y. Kuo and Aline K. Wong, ed. pp. 39-61. Singapore University Press.

Wong, James Y.K.
1971    "Planning for Church Growth in Singapore". In Urbanisation and Church Growth in Singapore. Church Growth Study Group and Graduates Christian Fellowship.

1973    Singapore: The Church in the Midst of Social Change. Singapore: Church Growth Study Centre.

Wu, Teh-Yao
1975    The Singapore Traditional Culture: Changes in Response to the Impact of Western Culture. Occasional Paper Series No. 15. Department of Political Science. University of Singapore.

Yang, C.K.
1961    Religion in Chinese Society. Berkeley, California: University of California Press.

Yeh, Stephen H.K., ed.
1975    Public Housing in Singapore: A Multi-disciplinary Study. Singapore: Singapore University Press.

Yeh, Stephen H.K. and Tan Soo Lee
1975    "Satisfaction with Living Conditions". In Public Housing in Singapore: A Multi-disciplinary Study. Stephen H.K. Yeh, ed. pp. 214-239. Singapore University Press.

Yeung, Yue-man and Stephen H.K. Yeh

1975a    "A Review of Neighbourhoods and Neighbouring Practices".
         In *Public Housing in Singapore. A Multi-disciplinary Study*.
         Stephen H.K. Yeh, ed.  pp. 262-280. Singapore University
         Press.

1975b    "Life Styles compared: Squatters and Public Housing Re-
         sidents". In *Public Housing in Singapore. A Multi-disciplinary
         Study*. Stephen H.K. Yeh, ed.   pp. 302-324. Singapore
         University Press.

You, Poh Seng

1970     "The Population of Singapore, 1966". In *Analysis of an
         Asian Society — Singapore*.   Riaz Hassan and Joseph B.
         Tamney, ed. pp. 23-76. University of Singapore.

# Index